KORI DE LEON

UPHELD

MEETING OUR TRUSTWORTHY
GOD THROUGH ISAIAH
A **6-WEEK** BIBLE
STUDY EXPERIENCE

ivp
Bible
Studies

An imprint of InterVarsity Press
Downers Grove, Illinois

InterVarsity Press
P.O. Box 1400 | Downers Grove, IL 60515-1426
ivpress.com | email@ivpress.com

InterVarsity Press® is the publishing division of InterVarsity Christian Fellowship/USA®. For more information, visit intervarsity.org.

Scripture quotations, unless otherwise noted, are from The Holy Bible, English Standard Version, copyright © 2001 by Crossway Bibles, a division of Good News Publishers. Used by permission. All rights reserved.

While any stories in this book are true, some names and identifying information may have been changed to protect the privacy of individuals.

Published in association with the literary agent Don Gates of The Gates Group, www.the-gates-group.com.

The publisher cannot verify the accuracy or functionality of website URLs used in this book beyond the date of publication.

Cover design and interior composite illustrations: David Fassett
Interior design: Daniel van Loon
Cover images: Getty Images: © oxygen, © haushe, © Tatiana Maksimova, © seamartini
           Rawpixel: Large Orange Lily (1786) by John Edwards

ISBN 978-1-5140-0772-3 (print) | ISBN 978-1-5140-0773-0 (digital)

Printed in the United States of America ∞

31 30 29 28 27 26 25 24 | 13 12 11 10 9 8 7 6 5 4 3 2 1

CONTENTS

WELCOME

Dear friend,

I am thrilled that you've decided to join me on the transformative journey of encountering the trustworthy God of Isaiah!

I believe we can identify with the Israelites who were walking through difficult days, yearning for assurance and the comforting words of God: "Fear not, for I am with you; be not dismayed, for I am your God; I will strengthen you, I will help you, I will uphold you with my righteous right hand" (Isaiah 41:10).

In these challenging times, we find ourselves surrounded by confusion and anxiety amid political unrest, a global pandemic, inflation, and a world that is drifting further away from a Christian worldview. Perhaps you were drawn to this Bible study because you are in an overwhelming season of life. Or maybe you are simply seeking relief from the weight of your daily concerns by discovering how to walk more in the burden-bearing grace of God. My heart is with you, as I can relate to both!

It is easy to fall into subtle, dark thoughts that we are all alone and without help in this world. As a result, we may develop habits of trying to manage everything in our own strength or anxiously looking around us for help. However, as time passes, the weight of fear wears us down, leaving us restless throughout the night, draining our energy, and leaving us feeling weary and faint.

In my early twenties, when I encountered the gospel and began my relationship with Jesus Christ, his Word spoke to my anxious heart and began unraveling this chain reaction of wrong thoughts. It became clear to me that we were all once separated from God and left without hope in the world. However, as believers in Jesus Christ, we have entered into a covenant relationship with God (Ephesians 2:12-13). The Lord has a special love and care for his people, which is revealed in Isaiah 40–48, where he assures us that we are not alone in this world. The Lord will be with us when we walk through the overwhelming waters of life. He will strengthen us to be his witnesses in a dark era. And he will bring us safely home. Why? He is faithful to his people, who are precious to him!

Knowing and trusting God is our new reality, and each of us is on a journey of learning how to walk in the comfort and confidence of Christ each day. The challenges we face are diverse and complex. We seek strength to nurture our young children and care for aging parents, wisdom to navigate the tumultuous middle

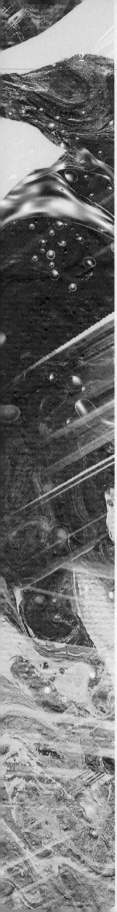

school and teenage years, and support as we walk through seasons of singleness. When battling sin, temptation, and the worry that God will forget us, we need hope and perseverance. We long for healing in fractured relationships, deliverance from the adversaries who oppose us, and so much more.

I've discovered that Isaiah 40–48 is a treasure trove for developing the habit of calling out to God and walking confidently in the help he provides. In these pages, God intimately enters into the hardships of his people, revealing his stunning character. And he presents us with a comprehensive catalog of comforts that address the various struggles we encounter in this fallen world. In other words, God does not simply say, "Do not fear; I will help you." He graciously showcases a gallery of specific ways he will uphold us. And are you ready for this? The Lord beautifully envelops his promises in poetic words, painting vivid images like stars and eagles for us to behold with our eyes as we go about our day. As we picture and ponder God's promises, we will find comfort and strength for our souls.

Each week's study begins with a group session, including a video where I share key concepts; then the group will explore the Scripture together. Five individual studies follow.

Through this study, we will learn a practical approach to putting off old habits of fear and seeking help from inadequate substitutes for God. And we learn how to walk in new patterns of calling out to God and waiting with humble expectation for the help he provides.

More importantly, Isaiah leads us beyond the hand of the helper to a deep love and adoration of his heart. The prophet showcases one of God's unique features: "From of old no one has heard or perceived by the ear, no eye has seen a God besides you, who acts for those who wait for him" (Isaiah 64:4). Did you catch that? Unlike false religions that demand human efforts to please their gods, our God finds delight in working on behalf of those who place their trust in him! God calls us to let go of self-reliance and the exhausting efforts of striving in our own strength, and instead to look to him as our provider, protector, and source of joy. When we call to God for help and wait with patient faith, we will see his wondrous works in our lives, becoming witnesses who share our stories of his glory, leading others to trust and adore him as well. And at our study's end, we will sing with Isaiah, "Who is like the Lord? There is no God like him!"

Eager to grow on this journey with you,

Kori

HOW TO STUDY YOUR BIBLE

Great are the works of the LORD,
studied by all who delight in them.
Full of splendor and majesty is his work,
and his righteousness endures forever.
He has caused his wondrous
works to be remembered.

PSALM 111:2-4

I am so excited to study the great works of God with you! Studying God's Word should not be a dry endeavor whereby we accumulate knowledge in the folders of our minds. When done rightly, it is the worshipful journey of beholding the person and works of Jesus Christ and becoming more like him each day (2 Corinthians 3:18). But a question people often ask me is, "How can I grow in studying the Bible?" I would like to introduce you to some steps we will take each day to equip you to study God's Word while we study Isaiah together.

Let's read and observe God's Word. One way to begin reading and observing a passage from the Bible is to ask the 5Ws and H: who, what, when, where, why, and how.

Let's look at the backstory. God revealed himself to specific people in specific situations at specific times. Understanding the backstory of our passage will give us a richer understanding of God's message.

Let's look through the lens of literature. God speaks to us in the Bible through different types of literature, such as narrative, poetry, proverbs, letters, visionary literature, and more. Isaiah 40–48 is almost entirely written in poetry, utilizing rich imagery to touch our emotions, imaginations, and intellects resulting in a transformative experience with God's Word.

Let's draw out the Author's intended meaning for our lives. We want to understand God's message rather than create the meaning ourselves. Therefore, we will contemplate everything drawn out of the passage and identify what it meant to God's original audience. We are not exiles in Babylon, but God's character and our human nature do not change. Therefore, we can draw out timeless principles to apply to our lives today!

Let's see how this passage points to Jesus Christ and the gospel of grace! In Luke 24:44-48, Jesus teaches that all the Scriptures point to him! Both the Old and New Testaments point to the life, death, and resurrection of Jesus Christ. And this, of course, is the *gospel*. The New Testament quotes Isaiah more than any other Old Testament prophet. Therefore, at the end of each week, we will reflect on how Isaiah's message ultimately points forward to the person and work of Jesus Christ on our behalf.

Let's be transformed by putting off the old and putting on the new. Let's not stay the same. Let's grow together by participating in God's transforming work. We will do this by putting off our old sinful life patterns, like taking off yesterday's clothes. And we will put on the new attitudes and actions that reflect the character of Christ!

HOW TO USE THIS BOOK

Whether you are engaging in this study with a large group, a small group, in a coffee shop with a friend, or by yourself in your favorite chair, here are some helpful suggestions.

FOR THE GROUP SESSION

Set aside a designated day and time for a weekly gathering—in person or virtually—for the next six weeks. The content (video and discussion) will take about an hour, but I recommend allowing some additional time for a check-in or to share prayer requests.

The videos are accessed through the QR code in the book. These videos were created with a group in mind—that you would watch the video together and then immediately engage in the content that follows. But it also means that individuals still have access, which is nice if someone has to miss a group gathering.

A FEW TIPS ON ENGAGING IN
A GROUP DISCUSSION

- Be willing to participate in the discussion. The leader of your group will moderate the conversation, and it helps them to have willing participants.
- Be careful not to dominate the discussion. We are sometimes so eager to express our thoughts that we leave too little opportunity for others to respond. By all means participate, but also make space for the insight of others.
- Be sensitive to the other members of the group. Listen attentively—you might be surprised by their insights!
- When possible, link what you say to the comments of others. This will encourage some of the more hesitant members of the group to participate.
- Stick to the topic being discussed and try to avoid "rabbit trails."

- Expect God to teach you through the content being discussed and through the other members of the group.
- Pray that you will have an enjoyable and profitable time together, but also that as a result of the study you will find ways to respond individually or even as a group.
- Remember that anything said in the group is considered confidential and should not be discussed outside the group unless specific permission is given to do so.

If you have time, a good check-in question might be to name a highlight from the last week of study—either from the group session or individual days. This study was designed so that you could still participate in the group session even if you haven't done all the homework, but—of course—I think you'll still want to engage with everything!

FOR THE INDIVIDUAL DAYS

Following the group session are five days of content for you to engage with during the week between group gatherings. I wrote this study with you in mind—so the content is meaningful but not overwhelming, and it's designed to fit into your normal, everyday life.

A FEW TIPS FOR ENGAGING IN
INDIVIDUAL STUDY AND REFLECTION

- As you begin each day, invite God to speak to you through his Word.
- Write your answers to the questions in the spaces provided or in a journal. Writing can bring clarity and deeper understanding.
- Keep your Bible handy—you'll be using it to look up passages. Sometimes I find it's helpful to look up a passage in another translation, and most often I use an app on my phone for that.
- It might also be good to have a Bible dictionary handy to look up any unfamiliar words, names, or places.
- A the end of each day, thank God for what you have learned and pray about any applications that have come to mind.

BUT THEY WHO WAIT FOR THE LORD SHALL RENEW THEIR STRENGTH; THEY SHALL MOUNT UP WITH WINGS LIKE EAGLES; THEY SHALL RUN AND NOT BE WEARY; THEY SHALL WALK AND NOT FAINT.

ISAIAH 40:31

WEEK ONE | TURN TO GOD FOR COMFORT

Group Session

If you were at my house, we would be seated in my living room, sipping coffee and enjoying God's rich design for relationships. What begins with curious introductions can blossom into kind acquaintances and deep soul connections in time. Though I am not with you in person, I am grateful to be able to join you through the video. And I pray for fruitful fellowship as you journey through this study together! In our group

 session, I will guide you through short readings with one another, followed by discussion.

View the week one video to begin this group session.

READ TOGETHER

The Book of Comfort. *Where can we find comfort and hope on difficult days? How can we exchange our anxieties and concerns for confidence in the help God provides?* Isaiah 40–48 answers these questions, growing us into worshipers of God who live confidently with him.

In the book of Isaiah, God's people were walking through tough times. They were no longer living in the glory days under Solomon's reign, but rather they were the rubble of a nation in decline due to sin. Like many today, people were faint of strength. They lived in an insecure world, and the faith of some flickered like a flame that could easily be extinguished.

Though God refined his sinful people through the fires of affliction in the Babylonian exile, he did not forsake them. His faithfulness shone through his special love and care for his people. And he entered into their hardship, awakening humble expectations for the help he would provide.

In Isaiah 40–48, God gave his people a catalog of comforts to carry them through the diverse difficulties they would face on their journey from captivity to restoration. Each form of comfort points to a greater help coming for believers in Jesus Christ, giving us powerful principles and promises to apply to our lives as we walk through this fallen world to our eternal homeland!

DISCUSS TOGETHER

I am eager to show you how God uses vivid imagery to uplift our hearts and showcase different forms of help that he delights to give his people.

1. Take a moment to read the list "Images in Isaiah" found in the back of this study. How do these pictures reflect God's unwavering faithfulness in helping his people?

2. Which pictures stand out to you as being helpful for people in our world today? Why?

READ AND DISCUSS TOGETHER

Recurring themes. Recurring themes surface in Isaiah 40–48, emphasizing the main points God wants to impress on our hearts. Let's discuss three messages we will continue to see throughout our study.

Turning to the God of all comfort. "Comfort" is a keyword and theme in Isaiah 40–48. God teaches us to find our help, strength, and comfort in him. He is trustworthy, and we can bring all our fears, heartaches, and needs to him. The apostle Paul echoes this message in the New Testament, saying God is the God of all Comfort, who comforts us in all our afflictions so we can comfort others. Let's look at a few examples together.

ISAIAH 40:1-2 | ISAIAH 41:10

3. What words and phrases does Isaiah use to begin his message with comfort and hope (Isaiah 40:1-2)? How should God's comfort affect our attitude and outlook in life?

4. What does being upheld by God's hand symbolize (Isaiah 41:10)? Why does this picture provide comfort?

Cultivating confidence in God's care for his people. When someone makes a promise to us, how can we be sure they will fulfill it? In Isaiah 40–48, God teaches us to lean on his character and care for his covenant people. God has a special love for those in a covenant relationship with him, and he is faithful. Though God refined his people through captivity, he did not forsake them. He upheld them and worked wonders to deliver, restore, and bring them home.

ISAIAH 41:8-9 | ISAIAH 43:2-4

5. What words and phrases are used to communicate God's special love and commitment for his people (Isaiah 41:8-9)? How do these words provide confidence in the Lord's care?

6. How is God's comfort different from the world's forms of comfort (Isaiah 43:2-4)? How does remembering God's care for his people change our mindset when we need help?

Knowing the incomparable God. We seek what we think will satisfy us. And we end up in captivity when we think someone or something *other than* God will ultimately make us happy and flourish. Judah was in a miserable condition because they exchanged the Lord for substitutes for him (Jeremiah 2:11). But through Isaiah 40–48, God fights for the hearts of his people using poetic devices like dramatic irony and sarcasm to mock idols that cannot profit. Isaiah also juxtaposes God's uniqueness with the worthlessness of idols to show how God alone can help his people.

ISAIAH 40:25-26 | ISAIAH 46:3-7

7. In what ways do both of these verses reveal the uniqueness of God? Why should this lead us to worship him?

8. In what ways are we prone to seek comfort and help apart from God? How can we grow in knowing the incomparable God and seeking him?

DISCUSS TOGETHER

9. Which of the three recurring themes interests you the most? Why?

10. When can you spend time studying Isaiah each week? In what ways do you believe prioritizing the study of God's Word can transform your current season of life?

11. What do you hope to develop in your life from studying the Bible within a community? Why is this important to you?

THERE HAVE BEEN TIMES when I would have loved an opportunity to do things differently. Like when I disrespected my parents by taking my car out—a week before I was a

HER WARFARE
HAS ENDED
ISAIAH 40:1-8

DAY
1

licensed driver. Maybe you never went driving as a fifteen-year-old, which resulted in a loss of privileges (also known as "being grounded"), but I'm guessing you've experienced regret. Maybe it was a careless word, a bitter response, a selfish act. Regardless, you wished you could go back. The morning of my sixteenth birthday, my dad tossed the keys to me as I stepped out the door. His gracious decision to lift my punishment deeply affected me. But far more comforting was his smile's joy, warmth, and forgiveness—a loving kindness that drew my guilt-stricken heart back to him. I learned that day that we don't get do-overs in life, but we can receive forgiveness. And that's the beauty of today's passage.

Isaiah 40 begins after the dark night of exile. The Israelites felt cast off and forgotten by God due to their sin. And there could have been no better news than hearing God speak tenderly: *your sin is pardoned*. God's message of comfort begins by addressing our most central need—forgiveness for our sins and reconciliation with him. And from there, every other gift of comfort will flow!

As you read through Isaiah 40:1-8, what do you observe?

List the different metaphors God uses to awaken our imaginations, touching our hearts and minds on a deep level. Which image stands out to you most?

The God of all comfort. Isaiah begins by using the poetic device of *repetition* to focus our eyes on the main message in Isaiah 40–48. The word *comfort* is repeated. And God instructed the prophet to "speak tenderly" to the hearts of the exiles.

What other words and phrases does God use to draw his people back to him (vv. 1-2)? How should this affect the way we see God?

An enthusiastic call to action. The Holy One of Israel had exercised judgment by exiling his sinful people, but he did not abandon them. Their exile was ending, and God was coming to deliver his people. Isaiah referred to a custom of some Eastern monarchs who would send a herald before them to clear the uneven ground in the wilderness that was covered by rock and sand. The representative would smooth out the roads in preparation for the coming ruler. With the voice of a herald, Isaiah called the exiles to action using *hyperbole*—an exaggeration of speech that communicated enthusiasm.

> Every valley **shall be lifted up.**
>
> Every mountain and hill **shall be made low.**
>
> The uneven ground **shall become level.**

● What is the prophet enthusiastically calling people to do in a spiritual sense? Why is this important?

God designed the world to be a theater for his glory. But we are inclined to take our eyes off God and focus on ourselves—sometimes in explicit ways and other times through subtle thoughts: *I will provide for myself. I will please myself. I will protect myself. I will lean on my own understanding and acknowledge myself in all my ways.*

Biblically speaking, this kind of focus on self is known as pride. Pride can take an inflated form of self-focus, as described above. But pride can also take the form of a morbid preoccupation with self: *I am not important. I am not good enough. No one cares about me. I have no help or hope in life.* God disciplined the Israelites due to the first form of pride. But many Israelites had swung to the other side of the pendulum by the end of the exile.

Some mountains of self-focus need to be laid low, and other valleys need to be leveled out through repentance. Then all eyes can be lifted to see the all-glorious God who calls us to return to a vibrant relationship with him!

A comforting contrast. When we see our sin and experience the consequences, we can be deeply discouraged by our moral failure and fallen nature. The exiles were there! But God entered their hardship, proclaiming the good news that he would help and deliver them.

In verses 6-8, God comforted his people using *parallelism.* Isaiah describes our nature using two parallel lines. Then he breaks the repetition with statements about the nature of God and his Word. The break of the rhythm delivers a more powerful contrast.[*] Read and reflect on the parallelism below.

The grass withers

The flower fades

> *When the breath of the LORD blows on it*

The grass withers

The flower fades

> *But the word of our God will stand forever*

- What contrast is Isaiah making between our nature and the nature of God? Why would this contrast help the exiles trust the good news that God will deliver them?

- Read Psalm 103:11-18. What is God's posture toward our fallen and fleeting lives? How does this enhance your understanding of God's message to the exiles in Isaiah 40:1-8?

---

[*]In my studies of biblical poetry, I frequently turn to *A Manual of Hebrew Poetics* by Luis Alonso Schökel (Rome: Editrice Pontificio Istituto Biblico, 2000). It's one of many excellent resources available that can enhance our study of Scripture, and I have relied on it several times in this study.

I love where our six-week journey in Isaiah begins! Believers in Jesus Christ have been eternally forgiven and set free from the dominating power of sin. But we will wrestle with remnant sin in our lives until we are perfected in the age to come. And on those days, let's continue walking in the comfort of Christ by (1) drawing close to our merciful Father who has compassion for his children, (2) repenting of our sin to God and the people we have offended, and (3) finding comfort in his eternal promise to help and uphold us.

TRANSFORMING LIFE PRINCIPLE

We can release the weight of guilt and shame by turning to God who abundantly pardons our sins through Jesus Christ.

- God uses powerful metaphors to communicate forgiveness, compassion, and good news for his people (Isaiah 46:3-4; Psalm 103:13-18). How can pondering and picturing these images in your mind draw you to God instead of away from him when struggling with sin?

- Repentance removes obstacles of sin that separate us from seeing and experiencing God. What aspects of your life would change as a result of repentance?

- What influenced you the most today and why?

DAY 2 — SILENCING DOUBT AND DESPAIR
ISAIAH 40:9-24

THREE IN THE MORNING can be a difficult hour. Stress. Anxiety. Doubt. Discouragement. Navigating relationships. Financial needs. Making parenting decisions. Caring for aging parents. For some reason, all the problems that feel manageable in the daylight can seem overwhelming to us in the night. What do we do when flooded with worry, fear, discouragement, and insecurity? Today's passage teaches us how to bring all of it—every last concern—to God.

 As you read through Isaiah 40:9-24, what do you observe? Consider how this passage's words, phrases, and structure are designed to remind us of God's greatness.

God is great, and he is good! The Bible teaches that God is glorious. The Hebrew word for *glory* means "weighty." God is weighty and significant, not light and insignificant. Have you ever wondered, *Why is God glorious?* The book of Exodus answers this question through two pinnacle revelations of God. In Exodus 3, God revealed the glory of his *greatness* through his name, "I AM." And in Exodus 34 he revealed the glory of his *goodness* by telling us that he is merciful and gracious, slow to anger, abounding in steadfast love and faithfulness, forgiving, and just.

So why is God glorious? He is *great*, and he is *good*! Moses responded to the revelation of God's glory by asking the Lord to take Israel to be his special people (Exodus 34:9). I cannot describe the privilege of being God's people better than an unknown Puritan who once said, "God's grace shall be yours to pardon you, his power shall be yours to protect you, his wisdom shall be yours to direct you, his mercy shall be yours to supply you, and his glory shall be yours to crown you." In today's passage, God teaches us to silence our weighty concerns by comparing them to the weight or glory of the One who helps his people!

God's goodness: Carried close to his heart. It is not hard to believe that God is greater than my problems. But I can catch my heart questioning his goodness toward me. Can you relate? Isaiah addresses our faith struggles by featuring God's goodness through a shepherding *metaphor*.

● What does the shepherd metaphor communicate about God (Isaiah 40:11)? How does this give people confidence to call out to him for help?

God's greatness: He sits above the circle of the earth. *Rhetorical questions are a literary technique often used in biblical poetry. Rhetorical questions do* not ask real questions; they are an artistic use of language that makes us stop and think about the obvious answer.

You may have used a similar method of teaching in parenting. One day my daughter came home discouraged by a situation at school. She seemed overwhelmed by her need for wisdom and guidance. I smiled because my husband is our church's family pastor and biblical

> I lift up my eyes to the hills. From where does my help come? My help comes from the Lord, who made heaven and earth.
>
> **PSALM 121:1-2**

counselor. I said, "Jade, who counsels the people at our church?" She stopped and thought for a moment, "Dad." It was precious to see her little mind click for the first time that her father's gifts and skills could also help her!

● What questions does God ask his discouraged and doubting people to pause and consider? How can these questions silence concerns in our minds?

40:12

40:13

40:14

40:18

40:21

God is alive and active, eager to work on behalf of those who call and wait on him. But sadly, we often strive in our own strength to fix our situations or pursue help from our substitutes for God. The prophet-poet leads us to turn from temptation and sin by using *dramatic irony* to laugh at the ridiculous nature of idolatry. He sets the stage for us as the audience, distancing himself from the idols he is about to expose, and then allows us to watch with transformative laughter as the absurd nature of our idolatry plays out.

● What do the ridiculous characteristics portrayed in verses 19-20 teach us about idolatry?

Paraphrase God's message.

● We can trade our daily concerns for comfort in God by . . .

 TRANSFORMING LIFE PRINCIPLE

Let God's greatness quiet our concerns.

● Our struggles can feel like giants that tower over us. What are some concerns causing you to cower in their shadow?

● How does your perspective change when you bring your concerns into the shadow of God's glory?

● Let's imitate God using dramatic irony to "put off" temptation and sin. Identify a substitute for God that you often turn to when you need comfort and help. Put it on stage, sit back, and consider what it does for you. Compare it to God, who rules, rewards, carries, leads, counsels, and teaches (Isaiah 40:10-17). How will this shape the way you respond to temptation?

DAY 3 — LIFT YOUR EYES TO THE STARS
ISAIAH 40:25-26

WE ARE NOT EXILES IN BABYLON, but we certainly experience times of feeling forgotten and insignificant as we travel through this fallen world to our eternal homeland. You may feel alone in singleness or as a young mom in the monotonous days of changing diapers. Maybe you are helping your teen who feels like an outcast. Perhaps you are lost in the middle years of life or feel forgotten as an older adult. Whatever season you are in, there are times when we struggle with feeling insignificant and forgotten by God. But in our passage today, Isaiah uses the stars as a storyboard to teach us how to put off discouragement and walk confidently in the awareness of God's love and intimate involvement in our lives.

 As you read through Isaiah 40:25-26, what do you observe? Give specific attention to how the teaching about God's greatness moves into lessons about his intimate involvement with his creation.

God's greatness does not mean he forgets his people. God's people rejected him and refused to walk in his good ways. As a result, they experienced the weakening effects of sin. The nation lost the honor and glory God had bestowed on them. Judah was exiled, weak, and humiliated. After being handed over to judgment for their sin, God's people felt forgotten, like insignificant outcasts among the nations.

● How is God different from the Babylonian gods (vv. 18-20 and vv. 25-26)? What phrase sticks out to you the most? Why?

● What does God want people to see when they lift their eyes on high (v. 26)? Why does this image provide comfort?

God calls us to lift our eyes to the stars, using them as a storyboard to teach us more about himself. The vast universe is decorated with innumerable stars, revealing that God is powerful and far greater than the things he has made. In other words, the Lord is *transcendent*. But he also uses the stars to teach us that he is intimately involved in creation and our lives. He knows each star by name, and not one is missing from him! In other words, he is *immanent*.

Read Psalm 147. This psalm was written after the exile, giving us a future glimpse of the Israelites after returning home, being restored, and celebrating God's worthiness to be praised.

● What verbs are used to describe God's work in the lives of his people (e.g., God builds, he heals)? What does this teach us about God's intimate involvement in our lives?

● How should God's immanence affect our outlook? What can we do to be more aware of God's presence in our lives?

Returning to Isaiah 40:25-26, the Holy One asks, Who is my equal? The psalmist and Isaiah answer emphatically that there is *NONE*! There are days when we feel like a distant star that has lost power and energy, becoming so dim that no one sees or cares for us in this vast universe. But the God who counts and calls every star by name is mindful of you. The One who upholds the vast universe by his power and understanding also upholds your precious life. He knows and understands your pain and will bind up your wounds. He has not forgotten you, nor will he fail you because he cares for you!

Paraphrase God's message.

● When we feel forgotten and insignificant, we can find comfort in our incomparable God by remembering . . .

TRANSFORMING LIFE PRINCIPLE

From the farthest star to your deepest scars, God is intimately involved in your life. He will not forget or fail you.

● Can you relate with the discouraged exiles who felt forgotten by God? Let's imitate God's use of dialogue. Write down the thoughts that often swirl in your mind and heart when you feel insignificant.

● How can lifting your eyes to the stars and remembering this passage comfort you when you feel weak, forgotten, and insignificant?

● Why is picturing and pondering God's Word an important discipline to develop?

DAY 4

WINGS LIKE EAGLES

ISAIAH 40:27-31

GOD IS TRANSFORMING US INTO PEOPLE who are enthusiastic to do good works (Titus 2:14). And we certainly see this truth worked out in the lives of believers in Jesus Christ. Our plates are often full of good works as we give our lives to serving the people in our homes, workplaces, neighborhoods, churches, and other communities. But can you relate when I say that there are times when I am just plain tired? What do we do when we need strength? Do we dig deeper and strive harder? Or do we spiral into emotional darkness? In our passage today, the exiles were weak and weary on the far side of exile. But God comforted them with an extraordinary message of finding new strength in him!

 As you read Isaiah 40:27-31, what do you observe? Give special attention to the words used for strength and power by circling them in your Bible.

Renewed from strength to strength. God spoke to his people using a poetic technique called *dialogue*. Interestingly, when poets use dialogue, there is not always a real conversation taking place. Instead, God uses dialogue to quote what his people are saying or to draw out the thoughts from people's hearts to address them. In Isaiah 40:25-27, what were the exiles saying, and what was God saying?

Thoughts/Dialogue of People's Hearts	God's Message to His People

● How does God's nature explain why he does not become weary or tired (v. 28)? How should this affect the ways we think about God's promises to help us?

Isaiah uses two more *images* to speak powerfully to our hearts today. The first picture is of a worker. God is always working and made us in his image to be like him (John 5:17). We get to participate in God's good works through our homes, neighborhoods, churches, and other communities. But notice a comforting contrast that is drawn. Unlike us, God does not grow weary—his power is inexhaustible.

Then Isaiah uses a second image to move his message forward to a stunning conclusion. He teaches us to look at the eagle, who changes from strength to strength in flight, and remember that the Lord imparts power to those who trust and wait on him!

● Reflect on the image of an eagle ascending from strength to strength as it progresses in flight. In what ways can this picture comfort weary people?

Friend, I picture and ponder the eagle in flight often, and I hope you will join me in developing this disciple because it is powerful! When we feel weak and weary, we do not need to fall into discouragement. We can call out to God, asking him to impart his power to us. And we can wait with humble expectation that he will strengthen us physically, mentally, and spiritually with the invisible power of his grace—lifting us up on eagle's wings.

TRANSFORMING LIFE PRINCIPLE

God imparts strength to those who call and wait on him.

● In what areas of your life do you feel mentally, emotionally, or physically exhausted?

● In what ways are you prone to strive through these situations in your own strength?

● How does God's promise to impart strength to his people encourage you personally?

DAY 5 | **COMFORT IN CHRIST**

THE PERSON AND WORK OF JESUS CHRIST are so grand that God designed history as one extended lesson plan, preparing us to see and celebrate him. After Jesus was resurrected from the dead, he explained that the Old and New Testaments point to his life, death, and resurrection (Luke 24:44-48). Throughout Isaiah, we have learned powerful principles for finding comfort and help from God. Let's take these habits to a higher level by pausing and reflecting on how they are fulfilled in Jesus Christ and the gospel!

READ

Find comfort in Christ's forgiveness. Isaiah is called the "evangelical prophet," and his book, the "gospel of the Old Testament." The Israelites were in a miserable condition in exile because of their sin. But chapter forty opened with God comforting his people through the good news of his forgiveness and deliverance.

Interestingly, the New Testament begins by echoing Isaiah 40 with a voice crying out in the wilderness, *Repent, for the King and his kingdom are here* (Isaiah 40:1-5; Matthew 3:1-4; Matthew 26–27). All people have been separated from God due to sin. But John the Baptist calls people to repent, removing obstacles that separate us from God so we can see and experience his glory. Jesus Christ came to deliver us from captivity to sin. He received ample punishment for our sins on the cross, canceling our debt and making peace between us with God. And on this side of the cross, it is stunning to reflect on Isaiah's words, *Her warfare has ended!*

REFLECT

● How does Jesus' fulfillment of Isaiah 40:1-5 lead you to adore him today?

READ

Find comfort in God's Word—through the gospel. Do you struggle with getting older? If your answer is yes, then you are not alone. Mortality is disturbing to many, resulting in a $60 billion anti-aging industry that continues to climb in profits yearly. We strive to look like we are staying young, but the truth is, our lives are frail and fleeting. Though God's people experienced their fallen and frail lives on the far side of exile, God comforted them with his eternal Word of promise to help them.

The apostle Peter, in 1 Peter 1:22-25, quoted Isaiah to show a higher fulfillment of this passage! After humanity fell from glory, all our lives became fleeting—like the grass of the field. We are here today and gone tomorrow. But God's Word is eternal. When people believe the Word of God—through the gospel—God causes them to be spiritually born again, giving them eternal life. "Though our outer self is wasting away, our inner self is being renewed day by day" (2 Corinthians 4:16) until we are perfected in the age to come. Perhaps we could say that God's eternal Word—through the gospel—takes fading flowers and makes us bloom forever!

1 Peter 1:22-25

REFLECT

● In what specific ways does God's comfort of eternal life change how you respond to the aging process in your life and the lives of your loved ones?

READ

Silence your doubt and discouragement with the supremacy of Christ. In Isaiah 40, God displays the glory of his *goodness* through a shepherd metaphor. He also reminds us of the glory of his *greatness*. In the New Testament, God's glory comes into full view. The Son of God put on flesh and became man. Jesus Christ is the invisible God made visible! The Gospels are filled with accounts of Jesus demonstrating his power over creation, sin, sickness, demons, and more. They also contain beautiful testimonies of Christ's goodness. He is the good shepherd who leaves the ninety-nine sheep to seek and save the one who is lost. Through the New Testament, we can continue to grow in silencing our concerns with the supremacy of Jesus Christ.

Luke 15:11-32 | Hebrews 1:1-4

REFLECT

- Which attribute of Christ's greatness and goodness comforts you the most today? Why?

FEAR NOT,

FOR I AM WITH YOU;

BE NOT DISMAYED,

FOR I AM

YOUR GOD;

I WILL

STRENGTHEN

YOU, I WILL

HELP YOU,

I WILL UPHOLD

YOU WITH

MY RIGHTEOUS

RIGHT HAND.

ISAIAH 41:10

WEEK TWO | TRADE FEAR FOR FAITH

I love the illustration of a puzzle piece to represent every person in the body of Christ. God has fitted us together with wisdom and purpose beyond our comprehension. Your presence in your Bible study is by design, and it would not be the same without you—like a puzzle missing an important piece!

I think it is safe to assume there are multiple times a day when stress or fear threatens to overwhelm many of us, stealing our peace and joy in the Lord. We may pick up a child from school and hear the news that she was not invited to a birthday party. Or we receive a phone call from an aging parent who needs help, and we are not there to assist. Or another friend gets engaged to be married and we feel forgotten by the Lord in our singleness. We begin to search our minds for the promises God gives us to stand on—but do you ever have days when your faith needs an extra boost? In our study this week, God teaches us two ways to strengthen our

 faith in his promises: we can be confident in his *Word* and *covenant faithfulness*!

View the week two video to begin this group session.

READ TOGETHER

Covenant love and faithfulness. Covenant is a central theme in the Bible. In fact, the Bible can be called the old covenant and the new covenant because the word translated as *testament* means "covenant." A covenant relationship is a special kind of relationship whereby a commitment is made to one another. As a result, a person's faithfulness or unfaithfulness is often discussed in the context of these relationships. In this week's passages, we learn that Israel is unique among all nations because God chose Israel to live in a covenant relationship with him.

Let's pause for a moment and recognize that this profound relationship between God and man did not originate with Israel but traces back to Adam, who regrettably broke his covenant relationship with God. God graciously responded to Adam's unfaithfulness with good news in Genesis 3:15. A seed or offspring would come from the woman who would crush the head of the serpent. And in Genesis 12, God moved forward with his plan of salvation. The Lord chose Abram, a moon worshiper who lived in Chaldea (ancient Babylon), calling Abram to leave his idolatrous life and follow the One true God. God made a covenant with him and promised to make him the father of a great nation. The people would have a special relationship with God, be given a glorious place to live—the Promised Land—and be a blessing to the world (Genesis 12:2-3; 15:18-21; 17:3-9).

The Lord began fulfilling his promise by growing Abraham's family into the nation of Israel and bringing them into the Promised Land. But in time, Israel followed the idolatrous ways of the East. The Lord exiled his people from the land but did not cast them off. And in our passages this week, we learn the extraordinary reason why: there are people in the world who are special to God—those who are in a covenant relationship with him. We will also see how Israel's unfaithfulness to their covenant relationship highlights God's faithfulness to them!

GENESIS 12:1-3 | ISAIAH 41:8-10 | ISAIAH 41:11-13

DISCUSS TOGETHER

1. What will God do to bless Abraham (Genesis 12:1-3)? How does being in a covenant relationship with God change Abraham's life?

2. God loves all people, but he has a special love for those in a covenant relationship with him. How does God help his special people (Isaiah 41:8-10)? Where can you apply these promises in your life?

3. How will God help his people when enemies come against them (Isaiah 41:11-13)? What should God's protection produce in us?

4. What captivates you most about God's covenant love and care for his people in the passages above? Why?

READ TOGETHER

Confidence in God's Word. In our passages this week, God also teaches us to have confidence in his promises by pointing to the fulfilled prophecies in his Word. One unique aspect of the Bible is the prophecies it contains. God inspired men to record his plans hundreds and thousands of years before they came to pass. Biblical prophecies are often described with minute details and then fulfilled literally in time. No other literature contains this unique feature! The reliability of the Bible is extraordinary. And in our study this week, God comforts us with confidence in his promises by pointing us to fulfilled prophecy in Scripture.

ISAIAH 41:22-24 | ISAIAH 46:8-10

DISCUSS TOGETHER

5. How is God different from idols and false gods in both verses? What does God want us to learn about him?

6. What does the Lord use as evidence for divinity (Isaiah 41:23)? Why
    should this ability lead us to fear the One true God and trust in him?

7. How can remembering fulfilled prophecies strengthen us while we wait
    for the Lord to work on our behalf? What promise of God would you
    like to trust more?

8. What affected you the most today? Why?

DAY 1

GOD USED IT FOR GOOD

ISAIAH 41:1-4

ONE MORNING, I received a phone call from a woman asking for help. She was working for a leader functioning in unhealthy and hurtful ways. We have all been the woman on the other side of the phone. Maybe you have been wounded by unhealthy leaders in your home or workplace. Or perhaps your child has been bullied while the school administration looked the other way. Or maybe you may have been disillusioned because of abusive leaders in the church and Christian organizations. We can feel utterly powerless when someone in a place of power mistreats us. Disillusionment sets in as we wonder, *Who holds the person at the top accountable? Where can I go for help?* God answers these questions in our passage today. A ruthless and aggressive nation oppressed God's people, but the Lord announced his promise to help them, giving us principles to stand on when people come against us in this fallen world.

READ ISAIAH 41.

 What observations can you make in verses 1-4? Give special attention to the Lord's courtroom language and challenge to the nations.

Bring your concerns to court with God. Israel had stopped calling out to God and relying on him. Instead, they began looking to other nations for protection. God warned his people that he would *stir up* the Babylonians to use as a rod of discipline. And history fulfilled God's prophecy when the Babylonians conquered Judah. But their seventy years of captivity were coming to an end. And now God would deliver Israel by judging Babylon for their wicked ways.

Chapter 41 begins with God calling Babylon to court. The Lord comforted his people by asking more *rhetorical questions.* As discussed in week one, God uses this poetic technique to make us stop and think about the obvious answer.

● Record and reflect on the Lord's questions to his people in Isaiah 41:2-4.

⬤ What answer does God want us to consider? How does this give
perspective to Judah's situation?

 Who stirred up the one from the east? *Stir up* means "to rouse,
awaken, or incite." In our passage today, God is the subject of this
verb. Read Ezekiel 23:1-27; Jeremiah 6:22-26; and Jeremiah 50:8-10,
41-46. How do these passages help you understand God's providential
work of stirring up nations to accomplish his good purposes?

⬤ Ezekiel 23:1-27. A parable illustrating the spiritual unfaithfulness of
God's people. The two sisters represent the two kingdoms of Israel.
Give special attention to verse 22.

⬤ Jeremiah 6:22-26. Jeremiah describes the coming Babylonian army that
would attack Jerusalem. Give special attention to verse 22.

● Jeremiah 50:8-10, 41-46. God describes the Persian army coming to conquer Babylon after Judah's complete discipline. Give special attention to verses 9 and 41.

God comforted his people by saying, "Who stirred up one from the east?" The obvious answer is "Me!" God had *stirred up* Babylon to judge and refine his people. But now God will *stir up* the king of Persia to judge the Babylonians for their wickedness. Verses 1-4 portray the panic in the air when the Babylonians realize the king of Persia is coming.

God closes the section by reminding his people that he is not a spectator of world events: "I the LORD, the first, and with the last; I am he." He is the Lord of history. Even though the peoples' lives seem out of control, God is providentially working in the hearts of rulers, nations, and people to bring about his good purposes in our lives and the world.

Friend, the principle in this passage has dramatically transformed the grid through which I see my world and my daughter's world. Instead of feeling helpless, hopeless, and overwhelmed when people come against me or someone I love, I have found the confidence to trust that God is in our midst, and he has not fallen asleep on the job! While he may use others to refine us or move us in a direction where he wants us to go, he *always* addresses their sin and restores us again.

Paraphrase God's message to the Israelites.

TRANSFORMING LIFE PRINCIPLE

Rest assured, God addresses the sin of both the refined and the refiner.

● What did you learn about God in our passage today?

● Can you think of a situation when you were mistreated by people more powerful than you? How would you respond differently after studying today's passage?

● How can this passage help you "put off" retaliation and "put on" love and kindness toward your enemy, leaving room for God to avenge you (Romans 12:18-20)?

MANY OF US HAVE WALKED THROUGH deeply painful experiences in this fallen world. And the frustrating aspect of trauma is that it does not

> **FEAR NOT, I**
> **WILL HELP YOU**
> ISAIAH 41:5-10
>
> **DAY**
> **2**

allow us to move on easily. Instead of walking through present-day struggles with an average level of concern, our anxiety can be heightened because it is compounded on stress that has been stored for years. I am eager to show you through our passage today that God provides powerful truths to use like anchors for our soul until waves of anxiety subside. The Israelites had been through dark and difficult years of captivity. But God entered into their hardship speaking stunning words concerning his special love and unparalleled help for those who belong to him. Let's look at them together!

As you read through Isaiah 41:5-10, what do you observe? Circle the words used to describe Babylon's fear and frantic efforts to find strength and help from idols.

A people special to God. The ruthless nation that terrified and crushed God's people will themselves be terrified when God's judgment comes through the Persian army. "*But You.*" God uses the word "but" to draw a *big* contrast between Israel and Babylon.

● Read Isaiah 41:5-10. What contrast does the Lord want us to see? What should this contrasting truth produce in us?

Isaiah 41:5-7

Isaiah 41:8-10

God also comforted the exiles by reminding them how precious they are to him. When people come against us, we often feel weak and dishonored. Consider the child who is left alone at the lunch table because the queen bee leads everyone to get up and leave when she sits down, or the widow who is taken advantage of by others, and, of course, the whole gamut of people who have been physically or emotionally abused—all examples of people who can be left feeling unloved and dishonored. The Israelites were in that place. The glorious nation had become defeated and undesirable. But it is beautiful to see that God restored their sense of dignity by reminding them of who they are to him!

> *Blessed is the nation whose God is the Lord, the people whom he has chosen as his heritage!*
>
> PSALM 33:12

- Spend some time reflecting on the warm and personal words God uses for his people (vv. 8-9). How might these words comfort and restore dignity to people dishonored and oppressed?

Chosen

Friend

Servant

Not cast off

God speaks an extraordinary message in our passage today: "Fear not, for I am with you; be not dismayed, for I am your God; I will strengthen you, I will help you, I will uphold you with my righteous right hand." We are called to put off fear and dread like yesterday's old clothes. And then put on the comfort and confidence that God will strengthen, help, and uphold us.

But how do we describe the experience of living in a close relationship with an invisible God who is upholding us each day? Once again, poetry proves to be helpful! God inspired Isaiah to use the *image* of being held by God's hand. Pause and picture this image in your mind.

● What does holding someone's hand communicate (v. 10)?

● I love how Isaiah describes God's hand as *righteous*. God is not wicked; he always acts in accordance with what is right and good. How does God's *righteous* hand strengthen your trust in the One who promises to help and uphold you?

TRANSFORMING LIFE PRINCIPLE

Amid life's challenges, believers in Jesus Christ can rest in God's covenant love and devotion to us.

● Like the Israelites, we too have experienced difficult seasons. However, by embracing the truths in Isaiah 40–48, we can begin the progressive journey toward healing and wholeness. Take some time to journal about fears that have shaped your past or anxiety that is currently affecting you in the present.

● How are you personally comforted by the warm words and personal names God uses for his people? Which one meant the most to you today and why?

● In what ways will picturing the image of God *upholding you by his righteous right hand* comfort and strengthen you when you feel afraid?

DAY 3
RENEWED BY STREAMS OF GRACE
ISAIAH 41:11-20

WE ALL LONG FOR PEACEFUL DAYS when enjoying the good life with God is relatively easy. But there are seasons when we are pressed, yet not crushed; perplexed, but not in despair; persecuted, but not abandoned; struck down, but not destroyed. You know . . . those seasons. Bobby and I emerged from one of those seasons mentally, emotionally, and physically exhausted. We were grateful God upheld us as we passed through the fires of standing for righteousness, exposing darkness, and accepting the cost. But it was one of the hardest years of our adult life. While I would not want to relive those days, we saw God work in three astonishing ways described in our passage today. God encouraged the Israelites that he would help them by working justice on their behalf, strengthening them for greater kingdom works, and renewing them by streams of grace!

 As you read Isaiah 41:11-20, what do you observe? Give special attention to the repeating words and phrases "Behold," "Fear not," and "I am the one that helps you."

 God weakens the arrogant. Babylon humbled the sinful Israelites, leaving them feeling like insignificant, weak worms. But Isaiah comforted God's people by reminding them of God's justice, which is like two sides of a coin: God humbles the arrogant, and he vindicates the oppressed. The prophet uses the *exclamation* "Behold" twice to transition us from the first aspect of God's justice to the second:

- "Behold," I will help you by scattering your enemies (verses 11-14), and
- "Behold," I will strengthen you to change the world for my glory (verses 15-16).

Out of my distress, I called on the Lord; the Lord answered me and set me free. The Lord is on my side; I will not fear. What can man do to me? The Lord is on my side as my helper; I shall look in triumph on those who hate me.

PSALM 118:5-7

I love watching biblical poets use synonyms! Think like a writer for a moment. How can you use words to get your readers to slow down and hover over an important point you want to make? You don't want to sound monotonous using the same word and phrases. So you reach for synonyms— words and phrases that essentially mean the same thing. This poetic device allows biblical authors to slow down and hover with readers on a moment of worship, an emotion, and more. And as we see today, Isaiah uses synonyms to soothe Judah's crushed soul by pondering God's justice. In verses 11-12, Isaiah uses four synonyms to describe Israel's enemy and eight synonyms for the disaster God's judgment will bring upon them.

● Let's begin with the first section, verses 11-14. Record and reflect on the synonyms used to describe Judah's enemies and God's justice. How would these words comfort God's people in captivity to a ruthless nation?

Synonyms describing Judah's enemies:

Synonyms describing God's justice:

God strengthens the humble. "Behold" is used a second time to comfort Judah by considering the other side of justice. God teaches us to picture the *image* of a strong instrument for farming. A threshing sled was made of heavy boards with sharp metal points. It drove over the stalks of corn to break out the grain, leaving the husks to be blown away by the wind. In other words, God will scatter Israel's enemies and strengthen his people for kingdom impact (verses 15-16). Though the exiles felt weak, God would restore and use them again as vessels of honor.

● How do these passages grow your understanding of God's justice?

God makes streams in the desert. In Isaiah 41:17-20, change is in the air! The absence of plant vitality helps us understand the effects of sin in our lives. God's people had become a wilderness, but he used botanical images to describe his renewing grace.

● What do the figurative phrases "seeking water" and "parched with thirst" communicate about God's people (v. 17)? When have you been in a similar place?

● Who will transform the desolate places into fertile fields (vv. 18-19)? Why is this important to recognize (v. 20)?

Reflect on the botanical images in Isaiah 51:3:

   For the LORD comforts Zion:
      he comforts all her waste places
   and makes her wilderness like Eden,
      her desert like the garden of the LORD;
   joy and gladness will be found in her,
      thanksgiving and the voice of song.

● How do these verses help you understand God's work of renewal?

The Lord will provide for his people on their journey through the wilderness on their return home, as in the exodus. And he will spiritually renew their places laid waste due to sin. I love how God concludes this section of Isaiah 41 by saying, "That they may see and know, may consider and understand together, that the hand of the LORD has done this." You won't find water in the wilderness, and you don't find life apart from God. Streams in the desert are a miracle—a work that God alone can do! God teaches us not to be dismayed when we walk through dark seasons with oppressive people. We can call on him and trust that he will work justice on our behalf. He will strengthen us and transform our weary souls to be like the garden of God again!

TRANSFORMING LIFE PRINCIPLE

God weakens the arrogant and renews the humble with streams of grace.

● Write one statement that spoke to you today. Why did it stand out to you?

● How will the two sides of God's justice provide comfort when you are wronged and deeply hurt by others?

● We can emerge from difficult seasons feeling like a wasted place. How does picturing the botanical images in our passage today encourage you to turn to the Lord for help and trust that he will renew you with streams of grace?

HARD EXPERIENCES ARE MEANT to bring us closer to God, but they can also leave us struggling to believe God. We often hear crisis-of-faith stories in our small group

| BELIEVING GOD | DAY |
| ISAIAH 41:21-29 | 4 |

Bible studies when people share their testimonies. Perhaps you struggled to believe God's Word after having a miscarriage. Maybe you questioned God's promises during singleness. Or perhaps your children are questioning God's existence because he doesn't seem to answer their prayers.

Shortly after beginning a relationship with Jesus Christ, my father received a cancer diagnosis. One evening I was standing on the deck of our house at twilight overlooking an open field that seemed to reflect the vacancy in my life. Confusion swirled through my mind. *Why was God allowing this to happen to us? Why was he not answering our prayers for healing?* When I returned inside, still broken and confused, I picked up my Bible and began reading the book of Revelation for the first time. Over the next few months, I was amazed by how God used the fulfilled prophecies in his Word and promises of eternal glory to strengthen my faith for the difficult days before us. Interestingly, in our passage today, God leads his people into a similar lesson that I am eager to unfold together!

 As you read through Isaiah 41:21-29, what do you observe? Give special attention to the synonyms Isaiah uses for *prophesy*, such as *tell* and *declare*.

Only God knows the future. God calls our idols to court with him. What does the Lord challenge our idols to do to prove their divinity (vv. 21-24)? How does this highlight the uniqueness of God?

● God repeats the *exclamation* "Behold" to focus our attention on the life of an idolater. What does idolatry produce in people (vv. 24 and 29)? How should beholding this truth transform us?

After revealing the uselessness of the idols people seek, God proves his divinity by giving a detailed prophecy. God will raise up a king to conquer Babylon and help his people. And in chapter 45, God identifies the king by the name Cyrus. Isaiah wrote this prophecy about 150 years before Cyrus was born! The prophecy was fulfilled in 539 BC when Cyrus the Great, who ruled the Medo-Persian Empire, conquered Babylon and assisted the Jews in returning to Jerusalem and rebuilding the temple.

Isaiah's prophecies have begun to be fulfilled! Many of Isaiah's prophecies have been literally fulfilled through the person and work of Jesus Christ. Let's strengthen our faith in God's Word by considering a few examples. Read and record how Jesus fulfilled Isaiah's prophecies concerning the Messiah.

Isaiah's Prophecies About the Messiah	How Jesus Christ Fulfilled the Prophecies
Isaiah 7:14	Luke 1:26-31
Isaiah 50:6	Matthew 26:67
Isaiah 52:14; 53:2	Mark 15:15-19
Isaiah 53:5	1 Peter 2:24-25
Isaiah 53:9	Matthew 27:57-60

Isaiah's remaining prophecies are about the glorious future God has designed for his people! Though the circumstances that often cause us to question God are real and painful, the prophecies about our glorious future remind us of how short this life is and fill us with great hope of the grand life coming soon for believers in Jesus Christ (Revelation 22:1-3).

TRANSFORMING LIFE PRINCIPLE

Believe in God's promises; you will be blessed when he fulfills them.

● I shared about a time when I had a crisis of faith. What situations or circumstances cause you to struggle in believing God and his promises to you?

● When we struggle to believe God's promises, we can be tempted to drift or depart from him. Take a moment to look at the graphic "Overcoming Temptation" in the back of this study. Identify one way you are tempted to seek help and comfort in someone or something as a substitute for God. How can using the principles in this diagram assist you in resisting temptation during those times when you find it challenging to trust in God's promises to help you?

● Identify one fulfilled prophecy above that strengthens your confidence in God's Word. How has it shifted your thinking today?

I HOPE YOU HAD a worshipful week in Isaiah! God teaches us to "Fear not," for he will help and uphold us through every twist and turn of the journey. Amen, and amen.

CONFIDENCE IN CHRIST

DAY 5

In our passages this week, the Lord gave us two foundations to stand on when we need an extra boost of faith: he has a special love for those in a covenant relationship with him, and he is faithful to fulfill his Word. Given these truths, let's sit back and reflect on the glorious ways God has fulfilled his promises to help his people through Jesus Christ!

READ

God helps his special people. This week, we explored God's special love for those in a covenant relationship with him. We also heard the Lord speak with warm and personal words, describing his precious people as chosen, friends, and more. Ephesians 1 takes these truths to an even higher level! God always planned to bring Jews and Gentiles into one spiritual family. Those who enter into a covenant relationship with God by believing in Jesus Christ are called chosen, adopted as sons and daughters, forgiven, redeemed, recipients of the Holy Spirit, and more. Speechless!

EPHESIANS 1:1-14

REFLECT

● How do the spiritual blessings in Christ lead you to praise God today?

READ

The Holy Spirit transforms our waste places into the garden of God. In Isaiah 40, the Lord revealed another form of help that he gives to his people: he will transform our wasted places to be like the garden of God. In the New Testament, the Holy Spirit creates new life in hearts that were once hardened. And as believers abide in Jesus Christ, progressive fruit springs forth. Certainly, some areas of our lives are not wholly surrendered to the Spirit. The stewardship of our time, resources, and gifts may look like barren ground in the fall. Some of our marriages or relationships still look like waste places. But God calls us to participate in our transformation. And as we surrender these areas to the Holy Spirit, we will become more like a fruitful garden each day!

John 4:1-42 | John 7:37-39 | John 17:1-17

REFLECT

- Spend some time communicating your gratitude to God. In what areas of your life have you seen the Holy Spirit bring life and vitality?

- Write the areas in your life that are still like dry riverbeds. What specific actions can you take to surrender to the Holy Spirit?

- What people do you know who need renewal? Pray to God, asking him to open streams of grace in their lives.

READ

Confidence in Christ's Words. As we discussed this week, we all have crisis-of-faith moments. But God strengthens our confidence in his Word by giving us fulfilled prophecies in Scripture. I want to close our time today by showing you that Jesus Christ, the Son of God, displayed his divine nature by foretelling the future so we could also have confidence in his Word. In John 13:19, Jesus said to his disciples, "I am telling you this now, before it takes place, that when it does take place you may believe that I am he." Throughout the Gospels, Jesus foretold his death, resurrection, and second coming. Let's look at a few of his prophecies together.

MARK 10:32-34 | MARK 13:24-27 | MARK 14:12-31

REFLECT

- In Matthew 24–25, Jesus followed the prophecy of his second coming with a parable about living ready. How does this stir hope and urgency in your heart today?

EVEN TO YOUR OLD AGE I AM HE, AND TO GRAY HAIRS I WILL CARRY YOU. I HAVE MADE, AND I WILL BEAR; I WILL CARRY AND WILL SAVE. TO WHOM WILL YOU LIKEN ME AND MAKE ME EQUAL AND COMPARE ME, THAT WE MAY BE ALIKE?

ISAIAH 46:4-5

WEEK THREE | LIVE THE GOSPEL!

Welcome to week three of our study! Under the new covenant, the Lord is not only creating individuals who know and love him. He is creating "a people" who know and love him. I often marvel at the joy my ministry team experiences in doing life and serving together. When I pause to consider why these relationships are unique, I believe it is the power of the gospel. A special fellowship can occur among "a people" who are united in the gospel and advancing God's kingdom together. And with this in mind, I am eager to tell you that this week's study focuses on our shared mission.

Throughout chapter 42, Isaiah addresses Israel's failure to fulfill their God-given mission. But the Lord responded to their rejection with redemption. He will raise a faithful servant to complete his purposes for his people. And Isaiah begins to paint the portrait of God's coming servant—Jesus Christ—hundreds of years before his birth. On day five, we

 will pause to marvel that Jesus is using the church to fulfill his mission to be a light to the nations today!

View the week three video to begin this group session.

READ TOGETHER

The Servant of the Lord. A key theme in our study this week is the servant of the Lord. God created Israel, gave them a glorious mission, and called them the "servant of the Lord" (41:8; 42:19; 43:10; 44:1-2, 21; 45:4; 48:20). Israel rejected God and failed to complete their mission. But where sin increases, God's grace abounds all the more! The Lord will send a faithful servant to complete the work Israel failed to do by being a light for the Gentiles. The servant of the Lord is a significant theme in Scripture. And the central teaching on the servant is found in Isaiah chapters 39–53.

ISAIAH 42:1-4 | ISAIAH 42:18-24

DISCUSS TOGETHER

1. What are the positive qualities of the faithful servant who will come to fulfill the Lord's mission (Isaiah 42:1-4)? Why would these qualities give people comfort and hope?

2. How did Israel fail in their mission to be the servant of the Lord (Isaiah 42:18-24)? What sticks out to you most and why?

3. How does the coming servant reveal God's faithfulness? How does God's faithfulness change our mindset in failure?

READ TOGETHER

A light to the nations. Let's prepare ourselves to get more from our study by discussing Israel's call to be a light to the nations. The Mosaic Law said God would bless Israel if the people walked in the light of his instructions, using them as a light to the nations (Deuteronomy 4:6-8). But if Israel did not walk in his ways, God would hand them over to a foreign nation who would exile the people from the land (Deuteronomy 28:49-53). This, of course, is the reason Judah was in captivity. But Isaiah speaks about the work his faithful servant will accomplish, which we see taking place in our day!

ISAIAH 49:1-6

DISCUSS TOGETHER

4. What are two of the servant's goals (vv. 5-6)? How does this add to your understanding of Jesus' mission?

5. What does it mean to be "a light for the nations" (vv. 3, 6)? Why is light important to bring newness and transformation to the nations?

6. What does the Lord's declaration reveal about his heart: "It is too light a thing that you should be my servant to raise up the tribes of Jacob and to bring back the preserved of Israel" (v. 6)? How should understanding God's heart grow our desires?

READ TOGETHER

New covenant. Though Israel failed in their mission, God announced a new work he would do, resulting in songs bursting forth worldwide. The new things God would do point forward to the new covenant. Let's consider a few aspects of the new covenant that will be instrumental in accomplishing God's mission to be a light and transformation to the nations. The most remarkable contrast between the old and the new covenant is the internal work God will do in people's lives.

> JEREMIAH 31:31-34

DISCUSS TOGETHER

7. How are the old and new covenants different? Why is this significant?

8. How does the new covenant enable the church to be a light to the nations? Unlike passive Israel, why should we all want to participate?

9. Why do followers of Jesus Christ find it challenging to fulfill our calling of spreading light and transformation to the nations? What steps can we take to be equipped to share the gospel and make disciples?

HAVE YOU EVER BEEN DRAWN to someone because of their gentle disposition toward you? I remember watching my father tame wild horses into creatures that would

A FAINTLY BURNING WICK ISAIAH 42:1-4	DAY 1

gallop freely throughout our property and yet promptly come to be saddled up for a ride when he whistled. My father's strength was impressive. But it was his kind and gentle heart that had a drawing effect on others. Throughout the years, I saw many broken people stream to our house to find shelter in my parents' mercy—an earthly glimpse of what we will see this week.

In Isaiah 42, God addresses a deep need in his people's lives. Though he would release them from captivity in Babylon, they were still in spiritual captivity. But the Lord will raise a servant, the Messiah, to deliver people from sin. And in our passage today, Isaiah prophetically paints the portrait of the coming servant by describing his gentle disposition toward broken sinners.

 Read Isaiah 42:1-4. What do you observe?

● What is the significance of the phrase "my servant" (v. 1)? What implications does this have for people today?

● What does "He will not cry aloud or lift up his voice . . . in the street" mean (v. 2)? How does this verse reveal the servant's uniqueness?

A light to the nations. It is important to understand that God created the nation of Israel and gave them a glorious mission, calling them the "servant of the Lord" (Isaiah 41:8-9; 42:19; 43:10; 44:1-2, 21; 45:4; 48:20). But Israel failed to complete the mission to be a light to the nations. They rejected God and were blinded by their sin. God responded to their rejection with a gracious plan for redemption. The Lord will send a faithful servant who will heal Israel's spiritual blindness and complete the work she failed to do by being a light to the Gentiles!

A portrait of the faithful servant. Isaiah gives two beautiful *images* of the servant's gentleness toward broken sinners. The Hebrew root *ratsats* is used to mean "to crush and oppress." The term became used to describe oppression, violence, and the mistreatment of others. Isaiah uses it metaphorically as a "broken reed."

The second *image* is a "faintly burning wick." In Isaiah's time, the wick of a lamp was made from linen. A feeble flame that lacked oil could easily be extinguished. These two pictures describe the faithful servant as one who is tender to the broken and weak.

● Reflect on these two images by picturing and pondering them in your mind. How would the description of the servant's gentle and compassionate heart encourage the Israelites to approach God, even in the midst of their failure?

Interestingly, Isaiah 43:16-17 uses the same imagery to describe God's justice! God will snuff out the wick of the wicked who refuse to repent. "Thus says the LORD, who makes a way in the sea, a path in the mighty waters, who brings forth chariot and horse, army and warrior; they lie down, they cannot rise, they are extinguished, quenched like a wick."

Consider this with me: The Lord is the Lamb and the Lion. He will not snuff out the wick of those who humbly repent of their sin. He will come with gentleness and meekness to help the lowly. But the wick of the wicked—who reject him—will be snuffed out in judgment. The prophetic picture of the servant's justice will ultimately be fulfilled when Christ returns as a warrior to judge the unrepentant and bring all things in submission to himself.

● How does the servant's gentleness enhance the beauty of his justice (Isaiah 42:3-4)?

 The Lion and the Lamb. We are all broken people who have been wounded by our sin and the sin of others. Many of us long for a gentle person to love, help, and guide us. We desire a humble teacher to instruct us in the good life and model the way. It is beautiful to see the New Testament open with the portrait of Jesus, who displayed meekness—power coupled with gentleness. He did not threaten or breathe out violence. Instead, he came to serve others to the point of dying on the cross. And he invites us to come under his tutelage, reminding us that he is humble of heart.

● Read Matthew 3:13-17; 12:1-21; and Luke 23:1-47. How does beholding Jesus as the faithful servant grow your understanding of his character and ministry? What hope and encouragement does seeing Jesus as the faithful servant provide for you?

Matthew 3:13-17

Matthew 12:1-21

Luke 23:1-47

TRANSFORMING LIFE PRINCIPLE

Jesus' tender and merciful character encourages us to approach him with our weaknesses and failures.

● The Israelites' unfaithfulness led to their exile, resulting in their weakened condition. In what ways can you relate to the image of a broken reed and a faintly burning wick?

● How does Jesus' gentle and humble nature comfort you personally?

● In what ways can picturing the images in our passage today encourage you to approach Jesus with your failures?

DAY 2 | **WALK IN THE LIGHT** ISAIAH 42:5-9

Do you remember what it was like to live in spiritual darkness? For those of us with a prodigal past, it is certainly not hard to look back and see the blindness that once eclipsed our vision of God. It is not that we didn't intellectually understand that God is good and holy. The problem is that we didn't see or perceive God's moral goodness as beautiful. Holiness was distasteful because we loved the darkness and lusted after sin. As a result, we fell short of living in his good ways, sliding further into our sin and misery.

Now that I have walked with Christ and participated in churches, Christian schools, and organizations, I have also seen the spiritual blindness of religious people who do not have a real relationship with Jesus Christ. Though spiritual darkness takes different forms, it is the reality into which we are all born due to sin. But we are not without hope! In our passage today, Isaiah continues to paint the portrait of the faithful servant who will help people by giving spiritual light to the blind. The result will be the creation of a new people who shine bright like the Son!

 What do you observe in Isaiah 42:5-9?

● What is the significance of God's role as Creator of the universe (v. 5)? Why should this give us confidence in the new work he will do?

A new thing will spring forth. The Lord of history uses a literary technique called progression to tell us a story about the work he will do. Beginning with creation, God made the heavens and the earth, giving breath and spirit to all who walk on it (v. 5). Humanity sinned against God and fell into spiritual darkness in Genesis 3. But Isaiah announced that the Lord would give his servant as a covenant and light for the nations (vv. 6-7). The Lord is progressing history toward a new thing he will do, "Behold, I am doing a new thing; now it springs forth, do you not perceive it?" (Isaiah 43:19). And the new work he will do under a new covenant is to

turn on the spiritual light in people's dark hearts! Let's pause to reflect on
spiritual darkness. Then we will savor the gift of spiritual light.

●   What will the Lord's servant do to help his people (vv. 6-7)? How does
    the servant's work grow our understanding of the effects of sin in
    people's lives?

●   Why will the servant bring glory to the Lord's name (vv. 8-9)? How
    should we respond to the servant's work?

He will bring newness and transformation to the world. The
New Testament opens with Jesus speaking about spiritual light, "I
am the light of the world," and "I have come into the world as light, so that
whoever believes in me may not remain in darkness" (John 8:12; 12:46; see
also, Luke 1:79; 2:32; 4:18).

Read 2 Corinthians 3:12-18 and Ephesians 5:1-21. How do these verses
help you understand the changes in a person's life when they receive the gift
of spiritual light?

2 Corinthians 3:12-18

Ephesians 5:1-21

The apostle Paul vividly portrays God's supernatural work through the gospel in 2 Corinthians 3:16-18. He describes the condition of the fallen heart, which is hardened toward God and veiled in spiritual blindness. However, he announces the good news, "But when one turns to the Lord, the veil is removed" (v. 16).

When a person hears the gospel and repents—turning away from sin and turning to Christ by faith, the Holy Spirit removes their blindness. The eyes of the heart are open to see God's glory through Jesus Christ. And what is the result of light? God gives us the ability to see or perceive the beauty of his goodness, and there is no place we would rather be. Paul helps us better understand this miracle: "For God, who said, 'Let light shine out of darkness,' has shone in our hearts to give the light of the knowledge of the glory of God in the face of Jesus Christ" (2 Corinthians 4:6). When God created the world, He caused physical light to shine out of darkness through the power of his word (Genesis 1:3). Through the use of a lovely parallel, we learn that God looks upon the soul that has become a dark and empty void due to sin and says, "Let there be light" in their heart.

Paul says, "Where the Spirit of the Lord is, there is freedom" (2 Corinthians 3:17). Fallen image bearers live in bondage. But when God imparts spiritual light into our hearts, liberation follows! When our eyes are opened to see the beauty of God's holiness, we *want* to leave behind our life of sin and shame and run into God's glorious and dignified ways. The slavery of "I have to" is transformed into the liberty of "I want to" and the privilege that celebrates "I get to!"

Legalism is trusting in your good works to be made right with God. Licentiousness erroneously relies on grace to justify a desire to walk in darkness. But God's gift of spiritual light sets us free from both. It creates love in our hearts for Jesus, awakening a desire to become like him. When the light goes on, everything changes!

TRANSFORMING LIFE PRINCIPLE

Jesus can turn our failures into opportunities for forgiveness, renewal, and transformation.

● How has the gift of spiritual light transformed your life? Spend some time communicating your love and gratitude to God for this extraordinary form of help.

● Where are you still walking in the dark prisons of sin? What steps can you take to walk as a child of light with your good Father?

● What stood out to you the most in our lesson, and what made that part particularly memorable for you?

DAY 3

SING A NEW SONG!
ISAIAH 42:10-17

METAPHORICALLY SPEAKING, do you ever feel like your soul is a sad country song—reciting the same discouraging struggle over and over again? Life in this fallen world is not easy. But in our passage today, God teaches us a new habit for putting off discouragement and putting on the joy of the Lord. Though Israel failed in their mission to share the knowledge of God with other nations, he will send his faithful servant to complete the task.

The result will be songs of joy breaking forth in souls worldwide. God calls us to rejoice over his glorious works in our midst. And when we put this new habit into practice, we will remember that even on hard days, we have good reasons to sing!

 Read Isaiah 42:10-17. What do you observe?

In Isaiah 42:1-9, we studied the new work the servant will do. Today, God calls people to respond with rejoicing and singing. Let's pause and reflect on a few aspects of this new song:

● Who sings praise (vv. 10-12)?

● Where do they sing God's praise (vv. 10-12)?

● What is the theme of their praise (v. 12)? Why is this significant?

A zealous heart. Isaiah gives us two intense *similes*: a warrior and a woman in labor. Then he adds *parallelism*, repeating himself three times. Combining these poetic devices paints the picture of a very zealous God ready to act on behalf of his people! (As you reflect on the passage below, please note that Isaiah is rough with the pronouns. Verses 10-13 talk about the Lord in the third person. Then verse 14 switches to the first person).

> For a long time
> > I have held my peace
> > I have kept still
> > I have restrained myself
> Now I will cry out like a woman in labor
> > I will cry out
> > I will gasp
> > I will pant

God is gentle, humble, and patient, but he is also a bold warrior, fiercely protective of his children. To Judah he seemed silent for a long time, but God was present. And when their time of discipline had ended, he was eager to judge Babylon's sin, resulting in the salvation of his people.

● Why is it important to know the zealous heart of the Lord? How does God's zeal change your perspective?

When we call out to God for help and he seems to delay, our minds can drift to wrong thoughts—some that are so subtle we don't even catch our minds going there. We can begin to think God is indifferent, or he doesn't care about us or the wickedness in the world. And we can find ourselves tempted to strive in our own strength or look to substitutes in creation for help. But one way we can put off these wrong thoughts is to picture the inspired metaphors the Lord gives us today about his zealous heart for justice and the deliverance of his people.

These are the things I do! God used Cyrus to lay low the Babylonians—leveling the country and drying up their lands to deliver his people. God revealed his zeal for helping his people and concluded by declaring, "These are the things I do" (Isaiah 42:16). Though God used Cyrus to deliver his people from physical captivity, he has provided a far greater deliverance through Jesus Christ.

Jesus has delivered us from captivity to sin. We should respond by rejoicing and singing a new song! We will certainly travel through hard seasons, but God does not want us to get stuck in sadness. We should not drown in despair and the rivers of our tears. Even on our worst days, there are good reasons to sing.

I can testify to the power of putting this habit into practice. I awoke one morning only to face various disappointments throughout my day. As my heart began to drop into discouragement, I remembered this passage and paused to celebrate the gospel. Jesus has accomplished an even greater work of deliverance than Cyrus had. *Jesus has saved me from sin, Satan, and God's wrath.* It was not long before God's invisible work of grace transformed my dark perspective into a song. And the Holy Spirit empowered me to press forward with joy. Friend, even on our dark and difficult days, we can fire up our joy and be strengthened by singing the gospel!

TRANSFORMING LIFE PRINCIPLE

On challenging days, find solace in singing the gospel, reminding yourself that Jesus has saved us from our sins and failures and has made us new!

● Write down one struggle that causes you discouragement.

● How does your perspective change when you pause and reflect on the gospel: Jesus suffered for your pardon and defeated your grave. He broke your chains of sin and bound you wholly to him. He has defeated your night. He will help you overcome this life and bring you safely home.

It seems fitting to conclude today by getting our worship on! Take some time to listen to one of your favorite worship songs and adore Jesus Christ for his works on your behalf.

DAY 4
PRAISE HIS UNSEARCHABLE WISDOM ISAIAH 42:18-25

NONE OF US LIKES TO FAIL. We can feel embarrassed when we do not succeed in our pursuits and ashamed when we morally fail by falling short of God's character and ways. I remember the worshipful moment when I realized that God has always been with me—even during my prodigal past, faithfully working to move my life toward salvation (Ephesians 1:4). Saint Augustine described a similar truth in his famous book *Confessions*. Even during his sinful pursuits, the Lord was with Augustine, mercifully judging Augustine to bring him back to God: "I swept across all your laws, but I did not escape your chastisements, for what mortal can do that? You were ever present to me, mercifully angry, sprinkling very bitter disappointments over all my unlawful pleasures so that I might seek a pleasure free from all disappointment."

In our passage today, we see God's extraordinary wisdom displayed by how he responded to Judah's unfaithfulness. God is just and will judge his people for their continual rejection of him. But he is also gracious and will turn Israel's failure into a gospel opportunity for the Gentiles. When the servant's mission is complete, he will faithfully return to heal Israel of their spiritual blindness.

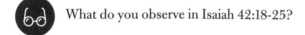 What do you observe in Isaiah 42:18-25?

● Who has become blind (v. 19)? Why is this significant?

● What was Israel's response to God's law (v. 20)? How do these verses reveal Israel's need for a Savior?

● How did God punish Judah's sin (vv. 22-24)? What does this reveal about God's justice?

Spiritual blindness and inner darkness. Did you know that there is an overarching storyline in the Bible? A unity of thought flows through all sixty-six books giving clear evidence that it was inspired by one Author (2 Peter 1:20; 2 Timothy 3:16-17). For this reason, different themes emerge in Scripture. One motif or theme that surfaces in our passage today is God's judgment of the spiritual blindness that has come on the nation of Israel.

● Read Isaiah 29:9-16 and Romans 11. How do these passages expand your understanding of God's judgment on Israel?

Isaiah 29:9-16

Romans 11

We often think of judgment as an end-time event, and it is! But the Bible also reveals a present-day form of judgment. Israel rejected God, and their self-will resulted in the judgment of spiritual blindness. Their inability to perceive God through his Word is metaphorically described as a book given to an illiterate man! The nation's hardened hearts were evidence of their *need* for God's servant to heal them.

Redemption: Their failure means riches for the world! The Gospels describe Jesus' ongoing battle with the spiritual blindness of Israel. The Lord is righteous, just, merciful, and faithful. And his wisdom expresses all God's attributes through the outworking of a beautiful plan. In Luke 14:15-24, Jesus used a parable to reveal God's wisdom in redeeming Israel's sin and failure.

The king invited the Jews to his great banquet. But they made up many excuses for not being able to attend. Finally, the host became angry and sent the invitation to the people in the streets—the poor, crippled, blind, and lame—in other words, the Gentiles. Israel's rejection of the kingdom would result in God bringing salvation to the Gentiles. But God will also be faithful to the faithless nation.

He will return to the nation before the end of the age, opening their eyes to see Jesus Christ as their Messiah, "Now if their trespass means riches for the world, and if their failure means riches for the Gentiles, how much more will their full inclusion mean!" (Romans 11:12). Paul concludes by worshiping God for his unsearchable wisdom!

TRANSFORMING LIFE PRINCIPLE

Trusting in God's unsearchable wisdom, we can take comfort in the assurance that He will redeem even our most profound failures for his divine purpose.

● How do our passages today enhance your reading of Jesus' interactions with the Jews in the Gospels?

● God's unsearchable wisdom is displayed by his glorious response to Israel's sin and failure. How can recognizing God's wisdom, as displayed through Israel's failure, inspire worship and trust in God during your own moments of failure?

 SEEING ISAIAH PROPHETICALLY paint the portrait of God's faithful servant—Jesus Christ—has been an absolute joy. And I am eager to take our reflections to a

BE A LIGHT TO THE NATIONS — DAY 5

new level today. Pause and marvel that the New Testament calls believers the "Lord's servants." Jesus is fulfilling his mission to reach the nations, and he is doing it *through the church*. Let me say that again and more personally—he is fulfilling his mission through you and me! With this in mind, let's reflect on our call to be *like the* faithful *servant* as we live on mission with him.

READ

Broken and faintly burning wick. Broken sinners are invited to come to
our gentle Savior for help. And believers in Jesus Christ are called to
represent Jesus by being gentle servants like him. Can you relate when I say
that this isn't always easy? Hurt people often hurt others. Broken people can
live in dysfunctional ways. Even the most patient person can reach their limit
when serving others and stumble like Moses, who struck a rock in frus-
tration with the Israelites. We can become exasperated by the sin and
unhealthiness of others. Aggressive feelings can stir in our hearts, tempting
us to strike out. But God calls us to continue to put off violence and put on
gentleness. We can grow in this habit by beholding Christ's gentleness in
Scripture. Our love for his beauty will inspire us to become like him. And on
a practical note—it is also important to maintain a healthy rhythm between
work and rest (smiling as I write).

   2 Timothy 2:24-26

REFLECT

● What does this passage teach us about the importance of being gentle
  and not quarrelsome as we participate in the gospel mission?

● What relationship challenges your Christlike gentleness? Take some
  time to pray, asking God to empower you to be like him.

READ

To give light to the blind. In Acts 26, the apostle Paul told King Agrippa about his story of receiving spiritual sight and the call in his life to share the gospel with others. Jesus sent Paul to open the eyes of the blind so people could turn from spiritual darkness to light, from the power of Satan to God, and receive forgiveness for their sins. With this in mind, it is stunning to pause and consider God's miraculous work through us as we share the gospel with the people in our homes, workplaces, neighborhoods, and other communities!

ACTS 26:15-18

REFLECT

● Write down reasons you can be passive or reluctant to share the gospel and disciple others.

● How does God's glorious work described by the apostle Paul inspire you to share the gospel?

● What steps can you take to be further equipped to lead others to the light?

READ

Sing the gospel! Isaiah pointed forward to the help Jesus would give
believers, resulting in songs breaking forth worldwide. It is beautiful to see
the New Testament open with joy and singing in the air because the longed-
for servant of the Lord had come to help his people. Mary sang her praise to
God, "My soul magnifies the Lord, and my spirit rejoices in God my Savior"
(Luke 1:46-47). And consider the theme of her song with me: God's
faithfulness to help "his servant, Israel" (Luke 1: 54). The night Jesus was
born, a multitude of angels appeared to lowly shepherds also praising God
in song, "Glory to God in the highest, and on earth peace among those with
whom he is pleased" (Luke 2:14). The New Testament continues with this
teaching, calling us to be strengthened and built up by singing the gospel to
ourselves and one another!

    ACTS 16:16-40 | EPHESIANS 5:15-21

REFLECT

- As we go out to sow kingdom seeds in this fallen world there will be
  seasons of tears. We will participate in the sufferings of Christ. And we
  may even find ourselves wanting to quit and give up. But the apostle
  Paul teaches us to rejoice because we have good reasons to sing. What
  will this discipline develop in us?

- What does God's instruction to rejoice and sing reveal about his nature?
  How does this lead you to adore and worship him more today?

Rejoice

The apostle Paul reminds us that even when we are faithless, God remains faithful (2 Timothy 2:13). As you wonder at this marvelous truth, you may feel inspired to overflow this page with your heartfelt expressions of praise.

WHEN YOU PASS **THROUGH** THE WATERS, I WILL BE **WITH** YOU; AND **THROUGH** THE RIVERS, THEY SHALL **NOT** OVERWHELM YOU; WHEN YOU WALK **THROUGH** FIRE YOU SHALL **NOT** BE BURNED, AND THE FLAME SHALL **NOT** CONSUME YOU.

ISAIAH 43:2

WEEK FOUR | REST IN GOD'S GRACE

Welcome to week four of *Upheld*! One of the benefits of doing this study in a group is the opportunity to dive deeper together. During our time today, I would like to point you to a pattern that surfaces in Isaiah this week: God will repeatedly recall Judah's sin, followed by messages of God's undeserved favor and saving help. The Bible calls this *grace*. And we see God's grace immediately put on display. Isaiah chapter 42 concluded with Judah as a spiritually blind, reluctant witness for God. But when we turn the page to chapter 43, we find the Lord addressing his people with tender, gracious words! Take a moment to gaze upon God's grace by reading the end of chapter 42 and the beginning of chapter 43.

The Lord is Israel's only Savior, and he will help his people even though they do not deserve it. Let's preview the gracious messages you will see this week, followed with a discussion of God's grace.

Day 1: Judah was sinful and spiritually blind (see the end of chapter 42). Grace: God will help his people because of his special favor and goodwill toward them (opening message in Chapter 43).

Day 2: Judah fell short in fulfilling their divine calling to know and believe God, and to be his faithful witness to the nations. Grace: God will still make his name known through Judah.

Day 3: Judah rejected God and went into captivity because of sin. Grace: God will make a way for his people to escape.

Day 4: Judah burdened God with their sin and loveless religiosity. Grace: God will blot out their sin and create true righteousness through the Holy Spirit.

Day 5: The gracious heart of God that shines in Isaiah comes to full light in the New Testament. All people have sinned against God, but he offers us the free gift of salvation that is wholly dependent on his grace! *View the week four video to begin this group session.*

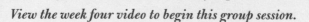

READ TOGETHER

Our need for grace. You may wonder why God continues to recall Judah's sin in our readings this week. I suggest that by doing so, God shows our need for his grace. The spiritual condition of Judah reflects the spiritual state of all people. Each of us has fallen miserably short of God's character and ways. Let's look at some Old and New Testament passages that reveal our need for God's grace.

Isaiah 64:6-7 | Ephesians 2:1-3 | Romans 6:20

DISCUSS TOGETHER

1. How does God view the best behavior of unbelievers (Isaiah 64:6)? Why is this important to recognize?

2. What are the results of being born with a sinful nature (Ephesians 2:1-3)? When have you seen sin's destructive nature in your life?

3. What does it mean to be "slaves to sin" (Romans 6:20)? What should we learn from this truth?

4. What do these verses reveal about our need for God's grace?

READ TOGETHER

What is grace? When Scripture uses the word *grace*, it often refers to God's disposition of favor, help, or goodwill toward someone undeserving of it. We will see this week that Judah did not deserve God's favor, care, and help. And let's be honest, neither do we. But that is precisely why God's grace is good news!

There was a time when the "undeserved favor of God" was the only definition of grace I knew, but it was a game-changing moment when I grew in a fuller understanding. The New Testament reveals that God's grace is not only his favorable *posture* toward his people but also God's *power* at work in believers to bring about his good purposes! Let's look at a few examples together.

1 CORINTHIANS 15:9-11 | PHILIPPIANS 2:12-13

DISCUSS TOGETHER

5. What were the effects of God's grace in Paul's life (1 Corinthians 15:9-11)? Why is this important for us to understand?

6. What does it mean that God is at work in you, "both to will and to work for his good pleasure" (Philippians 2:12-13)? How does this shape your thinking?

7. How does God's grace encourage you personally?

READ TOGETHER

Receiving God's grace by faith. How do we receive God's grace? A person hears the gospel message about Jesus Christ's gracious work on our behalf: Jesus lived the perfect life we failed to live. He died a sacrificial death to pay the penalty for our sin. And he rose again to bring us into a new life with him. It is believed that Martin Luther once described faith to be like an invisible hand that rises in a person's heart, taking hold of God's gift of salvation and making it their own. How can you tell when someone has a true living faith? The person believes God and responds to his word, resulting in repentance and a new life of progressive obedience to him!

ROMANS 9:30-33 | ROMANS 1:1-6. **Give special attention to verses 5-6.**

DISCUSS TOGETHER

8. In the New Testament, the apostle Paul said the nation of Israel did not receive God's gift of salvation because they tried to be made right with God by their own good works (Romans 9:30-33). What does it mean to receive God's gift of righteousness "by faith" (v. 32)? Why is this significant?

9. What is the result of true saving faith in a person's life (Romans 1:5)? What does this look like in your life?

10. What impacted you the most from our guided readings and discussion? Why?

THERE HAVE BEEN TIMES when I felt like I would be crushed by the heavy pressures of the world on my shoulders. When I looked for help,

WITH YOU THROUGH WATERS ISAIAH 43:1-7

DAY 1

there was nowhere to turn. Can you relate? Have you walked through an overwhelming situation and felt alone? Or perhaps you were not alone, but the people in your life could not help you when you needed them the most. Scripture reveals that even our most loyal companions can fail us for at least two reasons—spiritual warfare and the weakness of people's flesh.

Jesus can relate! He knows what it feels like to have the world's weight on his shoulders. When he was in the Garden of Gethsemane, he was overwhelmed with grief, troubled like never before in his earthly life as he saw the cross on the horizon. He asked his disciples to stay awake and pray, but they all fell asleep. Waking them, Jesus asked, "Could you not watch with me one hour?" (Matthew 26: 40). After acknowledging the weakness of fallen humanity's nature—*the spirit is willing to help, but human flesh is weak*—Jesus returned a second time to find his disciples asleep. This time he did not even wake them. Instead, he pressed into the One who does not grow weary and is *able* to carry our burdens—the One who is a steadfast, faithful Friend. Today's passage teaches us how to emulate Jesus by trusting the Lord when we are overwhelmed.

 Read Isaiah 43:1-7. What do you observe?

● Judah was sinful and spiritually blind (see Isaiah 42:14-25). What expressions of undeserved favor, goodwill, and help are shown to Judah (43:1-7)?

● What does this teach us about God's character?

 Because I love you. Today's passage will radiate with more beauty in light of some backstory, so let's look at it together. In the book of Deuteronomy, Moses instructed Israel not to become prideful when God blessed them in the Promised Land. The Lord chose Israel out of all the people of the earth to be his treasured possession, but he wanted them to remember their humble beginnings.

● Read Deuteronomy 7:6-9. What does God want his people to remember about his reasons for choosing them?

   God chose Israel because . . . | God did not choose Israel based on . . .

● Why would God's election and covenantal love comfort the exiles? How
   should this change our perspective?

God's people were not bound to him by their good works or inherent
greatness. On the contrary, they were bound to him because he freely chose
to set his affections on them. God's election and a special love for his people
are foundational to understanding the stunning message he delivers to the
exiles today!

The waters would have tumbled us. Judah was sinful and spiritually blind (see the end of Isaiah 42). They were in exile because of
their sin. But God would still help them—even though they did not deserve
it—because he has a special favor and love for those who are in a covenant
relationship with him. I am eager to show you how Isaiah masterfully used
poetry to speak gracious words to overwhelmed hearts.

The prophet begins with pictures of elemental dangers. But notice how
he combines them into *groups of images*. Isaiah describes the waters growing
higher and higher, allowing us to feel the increasing pressure of life. That

If the Lord had not been on our side . . . the waters would have engulfed us.

PSALM 124:1, 4 HCS

would seem to be enough, right? Nope. He continues to layer on a second image of flames increasing into a consuming fire! By coupling these pictures, he identifies with people who are overwhelmed by life's pressures and hardships.

Pause to reflect on the groups of images used in this passage:

> When you pass through the waters
>> And through the rivers
> When you walk through the fire
>> And the flames

● What promises does God make to his people who are walking through perils in this fallen world (vv. 1-7)?

● How should this shape the way we respond during difficulties?

My ministry hosts events for women and teens each year. Partnering with many people to host these gatherings is a joy. But there are many moving parts, and there have been times when key leaders could not fulfill their roles due to unexpected hardships. The first time, I felt utterly overwhelmed. My heart became anxious as I thought of everything on my plate. My mind began to swirl with confusion. Stress gripped my body. Overwhelmed? Yes. Feeling like I was drowning? Definitely. But as I began to call out to God, he raised another leader to help, and to my surprise, she had specific gifts I did not realize we would need for the coming growth.

The next time we had to pivot quickly and overwhelming waters began to rise in my soul, I remembered this passage and put it into practice. As I pondered and pictured God's promise to help me, the rising waters of stress began to slow down and eventually subside. After seeing the Lord's faithfulness time and time again, I have become stronger and more stable in my service to him. I share this testimony to encourage you. We can be confident that God is with us and will help us through the overwhelming waters of life because he has a special love for those in a covenant relationship with him!

TRANSFORMING LIFE PRINCIPLE

Remembering God's election and covenant love will provide us with confidence that he is present and ready to help us through every trial.

- Isaiah grouped images of elemental dangers for us to identify with when we feel overwhelmed. As you ponder these pictures, what situations come to mind?

- Jesus is a sympathetic high priest because he has shared in our sufferings (Hebrews 4:15-16). How does his overwhelming trial in the Garden of Gethsemane encourage you to draw near to him for help in your time of need?

● How will God's promises help you grow in "putting off" fear and
"putting on" faith when you feel overwhelmed?

CAN YOU RECALL SEASONS OF LIFE when
you felt the gnawing sense of meaninglessness
described by Solomon in Ecclesiastes? You may
be in one of those seasons now. Perhaps you are
struggling with purposelessness during singleness. Or you may be a new
mom struggling with the mundane routine of changing diapers. Or perhaps
you feel lost in the empty nest season. These days come for each of us. And
when they do, we can take hold of God's comfort in our passage today. The
Lord has created us for a life filled with rich meaning and purpose!

 What do you observe in Isaiah 43:8-13?

● What does it mean that God created people for "my glory" (v. 7)? Why
is it important to align our lives with God's primary purpose for us?

● None of the false gods could predict the future or declare prophetic truth (vv. 8-9). How is the Lord different from false gods (vv. 10-13)?

● What is the role of a witness (vv. 10-12)? How can this change our mindset when we feel purposeless?

God chose Israel to be *witnesses* of his glory! What an amazing honor and gift. The nation was given access to the one true God—who predicts the future, delivers nations, and works wonders. God's people were also called to make him known by walking in his ways so other nations could see his glory and put their hope in him.

Let's marvel at another glorious truth together. The Lord concludes our passage today by pointing to his eternal nature. Pause and be in awe with me: the one true God has been manifesting his good works from the beginning of time until now!

● Why does the Lord's eternal nature provide his witnesses with abundant content to share with others (v. 13)?

● How does this inspire you to worship God and be a witness for him?

To know and believe that I Am He. When we feel lost in our sense of purpose, let's pause, catching our minds and hearts from spiraling into spiritual disorientation. Let's remind ourselves of our purpose to know God and share him with others! After Jesus was resurrected from the dead, he gave believers the glorious mission to make disciples until the end of the age. And in Acts 2, the Holy Spirit clothed his disciples with the power to be his witnesses to the ends of the earth.

I have come to see that each season brings new opportunities to be a witness for Jesus Christ. As a young single adult, I sometimes struggled because I attached my sense of purpose to marriage. But in time, I learned to focus on my higher purpose by being a witness for Christ in the fashion industry where I worked. When my husband and I were newlyweds, we were witnesses to high school students through Young Life ministry because we did not have to hurry home to tend to our own children. When my daughter was born, I focused on being a witness to her through family discipleship.

I could roll on with the different ways we can be a witness for Jesus Christ during our different seasons of life. But the point is this: we have been given the deep joy of knowing God through Jesus Christ, seeing him work wonders on our behalf, and sharing his glory with others. This purpose does not depart from us during the changing seasons of our lives; it just takes different forms!

 TRANSFORMING LIFE PRINCIPLE

In times of questioning our purpose, find comfort in God who guides and empowers us with the Holy Spirit to be his witnesses during each season of life.

● You are called to be a witness for Jesus Christ! How can this grand purpose comfort you on days when you feel useless and your life seems mundane?

● Israel was a reluctant and passive witness for God. Can you relate? How are you comforted by God's promise to clothe you with the power of the Holy Spirit to be his witness?

● What specific steps can you take to be a witness for Jesus Christ in your current season of life?

CAN YOU RECALL BEING IN A DIFFICULT SITUATION and unable to see a path through it? I still marvel at the night when my daughter grew from hearing the

THE WAYMAKER
ISAIAH 43:14-21

DAY 3

foundational stories of the Bible—such as the exodus from Egypt—to having to trust God at her first Red Sea moment. A difficult situation had come upon her during a time when we "happened" to be reading a devotional on the names of God. The night her trial hit its most challenging peak, we "happened" to be reading an entry titled, *I AM Your Salvation*, reflecting on Exodus 14. The Israelites needed deliverance from their oppressors but had no way out. They were in a situation where the only one they could call on was God, who responded by making a glorious way through the sea (Exodus 14:13-14).

My mother's heart was overwhelmed. But I reminded my daughter that we are not a family who looks to money to be our benefactor, accumulating wealth for security and power. We do not seek networks with influential people for alliances and protection. The Lord is our greater reward and helper. And in our day of need, we would call to him. We walked in godly wisdom—humbling ourselves, calling on God, and waiting for him to work on our behalf.

Seeing God make a way where there seemed to be no way for my daughter to find relief from her situation and be brought to a broad and spacious place was amazing. We still marvel at the season when my daughter grew from hearing the stories about how God worked on behalf of his people to realizing he works in those ways in her life. I am excited to show you in our passage today that the Lord teaches us a similar message!

 What do you observe in Isaiah 43:14-21? Give special attention to the repeated phrases, "who makes a way" and "I will make a way."

● What does God want his people to behold (v. 19)? How should beholding his work grow us?

● What will result from God's saving work (vv. 20-21)? Why is this significant?

I will make a way. Isaiah used an *allusion* to the exodus, associating God's work in the past with the promise that he will do a similar work in the present. Notice that God teaches us *not to view his work of deliverance as a one-time event!* There will be a second exodus, but this time from Babylon. God comforted the exiles by promising to deliver and help them return home again, "I will make a way in the wilderness" (Isaiah 43:18-19).

● How would recalling God's past faithfulness strengthen the exiles' faith and hope in God's promise to deliver them again? Why is cultivating the spiritual discipline of remembering God's past faithfulness crucial in life?

● Read and reflect on Ezra 7:1-28 and 8:21-32. How do these passages show the fulfillment of God's promise to help his people return home under the leadership of Ezra? How should this grow our trust in God?

Ezra 7:1-28

Ezra 8:21-32

God's people were learning! They went into exile for putting their trust in princes, but they came out putting their trust in God: "The hand of our God was on us, and he delivered us from the hand of the enemy and from ambushes by the way" (Ezra 8:31).

> *Some trust in chariots and some in horses, but we trust in the name of the Lord our God. They collapse and fall, but we rise and stand upright.*
>
> **PSALM 20:7-8**

Earlier this week, I shared a story about times when I became anxious due to needing more help and resources in my ministry as it grew. One night I shared my concerns with my husband, and I will never forget his response. "We may not know the path forward, but we know the *way*. And the *way* is trusting God, so stay on that route." Bobby's point was powerful and ministered mightily to my soul. There will be days when we do not see a path forward, and those are the days to remember that trusting God is the *way*. He will uphold and guide us by his righteous right hand. We will see him as our Waymaker and emerge with new stories to share that will lead others to trust in him as well!

Paraphrase God's message.

>
> "
>
>
>
>
>
>
>   "

 TRANSFORMING LIFE PRINCIPLE

God will make a way when we see no path forward.

● List some times when you saw God work in your life in a way that paralleled the stories of the Bible.

● I shared several stories when my family could not see a way through a difficult situation. Write about a situation or circumstance where you have needed guidance or deliverance but could not see a path forward. How did you respond?

● God teaches us not to view his work of deliverance as a one-time event. In what specific ways are you comforted and changed by God's promise to be the Waymaker for his people?

MY HUSBAND AND I invited a couple who moved from New York to Houston for dinner one evening. At some point in the conversation, the topic of God came

FEAR NOT, MY
RIGHTEOUS ONE
ISAIAH 43:22–44:20

DAY
4

up. I asked where they were in their spiritual journey, and the husband said, "When we moved to the South, we started going to church to meet people because that seems to be what everyone does here." After we laughed together, he shared that he would like to begin a relationship with Christ but didn't know how to begin. Shortly following, his wife responded with an equally sincere answer that I will never forget, "There are some aspects of Christianity that I find beautiful—one being that Christians do not need material things to make them happy. But my struggle with the gospel is that I do not see myself as a sinner. I think I am a pretty good person."

That night, Christ's words in John 16:8 came alive for me at a new level. Jesus told his disciples it would benefit them when he returned to heaven because he would send the *Helper*. When the Holy Spirit comes, "He will convict the world concerning sin and righteousness and judgment." Pause with me and reflect on our need for the Holy Spirit to convict us of sin so we can be led to repentance and reconciliation with God. In our passage today, we see another cycle of God recalling Judah's sin, followed by an extraordinary message of his gracious plan to help them.

 What do you observe in Isaiah 43:22–44:5? Give special attention to how 43:22-28 focuses on the burden of Judah's sin and religiosity, while 44:1-5 is a tender word of hope concerning the help God will provide.

 Burdened by religiosity. The Lord recalls Judah's past unfaithfulness using *rhetorical irony* to capture the attention of his people. Rhetorical irony is when something said is in contrast to reality.

● What point is God making through the use of irony (Isaiah 43:22-23)? What does this teach us to avoid?

● How did Israel burden God with empty ritualism (v. 23-24)? What does this teach us about God?

● How is God's grace seen through his response to Judah (43:25–44:5)?

Fear not, Jeshurun. As we have seen throughout our passages this week, God's response to his people's failures is not what we would expect! He affectionately tells his disobedient people, "Fear not, . . . *Jeshurun*," a name that means "right" or "straight." Okay, we must slow down and marvel at this name together!

Some of us struggle with remnant sin that leans toward religiosity as the Israelites did, and others tend toward prodigal living. But listen to the comfort God provides for us all in this passage—*I am the One who blots out sin*, and a time is coming when the Lord will help his people by *pouring out his Spirit upon them*! At that time, people will confess allegiance to God from a heart of love and devotion. And in view of God's future work, he tenderly says, *Fear not, my righteous one.*

● How does the phrase "Fear not, . . . Jeshurun" comfort imperfect people who are in a covenant relationship with him?

TRANSFORMING LIFE PRINCIPLE

When believers wrestle with sin, we can find comfort in Jesus Christ, who is our righteousness.

● How do these passages help you understand our need for the Holy Spirit?

● How does God's gift of righteousness lead you to adore Jesus Christ today?

● In what specific ways will God's gracious words in this passage keep you close to him when struggling with temptation, sin, and shame?

THROUGHOUT ISAIAH 43, God recalled Judah's unfaithfulness and followed with messages of the help he would provide them. Seeing God's gracious work on behalf of his sinful people has prepared us to marvel even more at his amazing grace in the New Testament. I am eager to read and reflect on God's saving grace today. Let's worship together!

READ

Saved by grace. Like Judah, we too have gone the way of Adam, walking in his sinful footsteps. We cannot earn God's favor because that would require moral perfection, and we all fall far short of it. Though God is just and will punish sinners, he is also gracious. He delivered Judah from captivity. And he designed an even greater salvation from sin that is wholly dependent on his grace! Jesus accomplished all the work for our salvation from sin, Satan, and God's coming wrath, and we did *nothing* to earn it. We are saved by God's grace, not our good works (Ephesians 2:8-9). For this reason, believers will praise God's amazing grace for ages upon ages!

Ephesians 2:8-9

REFLECT

● Take time to reflect on God's salvation by grace alone through faith alone in Jesus Christ alone. How does this lead you to love and worship him more today?

READ

Christ is our righteousness. Judah burdened God with their loveless religiosity and unrighteous ways. But God comforted them with the gracious promise that he would one day create true love and righteousness in people's hearts through the Holy Spirit. We see the fulfillment of this promise in the New Testament. Jesus Christ lived a perfect life, earning a perfect moral record for us. By Christ's sacrificial death on the cross, he blotted out our sin. When Jesus ascended into heaven, he sent us the Holy Spirit. And the Helper has come to convict us of sin, lead us to repentance and faith in Jesus, and apply Christ's righteousness to our lives!

When we believe in Jesus, the Holy Spirit applies Christ's righteousness to our lives. We are justified or made *positionally* righteous before God. And the Holy Spirit begins to make us righteous in *practice*! As you pause to reflect on Christ's gift of righteousness, may you find great comfort in God's words from this week; fear not, *Jeshurun*.

JOHN 16:5-11 | 1 CORINTHIANS 1:30 | GALATIANS 3:13-14

REFLECT

● There will be many days on our journey through this fallen world when we struggle with sin and shame. How can these passages comfort you personally?

A third exodus is coming, and our Waymaker will bring us home. Judah went into captivity because of their sin. But God graciously made a way for them to escape once again, echoing their deliverance from Egypt. Friend, did you know the New Testament teaches that a third and greater exodus is coming? The church will experience God's deliverance in a similar but far greater way than the Jews. When Jesus returns, he will gather his people and bring us into our eternal promised land! God told Judah he would do a new work, pointing to the new covenant. God speaks a similar message to the church: "And he who was seated on the throne said, 'Behold, I am making all things new'" (Revelation 21:5). It will not be long before Jesus delivers us from this fallen world and brings us to a new heaven and a new earth. Until the third exodus takes place, we are called to advance God's kingdom in the lives of others today! Amen, and amen.

Rejoice

When have you experienced grace? Maybe you had a moment when God's grace was dramatically revealed to you, or maybe you've had people extend forgiveness and grace to you. Take a moment to wonder and rejoice in the gift of amazing grace.

FOR MY THOUGHTS ARE NOT YOUR THOUGHTS, NEITHER ARE YOUR WAYS MY WAYS, DECLARES THE LORD. FOR AS THE HEAVENS ARE HIGHER THAN THE EARTH, SO ARE MY WAYS HIGHER THAN YOUR WAYS AND MY THOUGHTS THAN YOUR THOUGHTS.

ISAIAH 55:8-9

WEEK FIVE | LEAN ON THE SUSTAINER

Welcome to week five of our study. I am eager to unfold more wonders in God's Word with you this week! In Isaiah 44–46, the Lord will lead us to higher places, giving us a glimpse of his governance of the world, and then come back down, speaking a personal message for our lives. We will be left with a stunning message of comfort: the One who upholds the world also upholds our lives! Given these glorious truths, why would we turn to idols that leave us carrying our own burdens when God delights to be our burden bearer? Let's prepare our hearts to get more from our study of Isaiah by discussing some concepts we will encounter this week. *View the week five video to begin this group session.*

READ TOGETHER

Sovereign. God has declared his sovereign rule over creation multiple times throughout Isaiah, and we will see it again this week. What does it mean that God is sovereign? Scripture reveals that God has the authority, wisdom, and power to uphold the world and govern all things toward his purpose for creation. Isaiah points to God's sovereign work of summoning Cyrus to conquer Babylon and help the Israelites return home (Isaiah 46:8-11). Let's take a closer look at God's sovereignty together.

    ISAIAH 46:8-11 | DANIEL 4:34-35

DISCUSS TOGETHER

1. What do Isaiah and King Nebuchadnezzar's statements teach us about God's sovereignty? Why is understanding God's sovereignty important for our lives?

2. How do you see kings and nations exalt themselves above the Lord today? How does Daniel 4:34-35 give perspective to these situations?

READ TOGETHER

God's good purposes. We may find ourselves grappling with God's sovereignty for several reasons. As fallen image bearers, we have a sinful inclination to control our lives rather than submit to our Creator. Others may wrestle with sovereignty because they have been hurt by sinful men or women who used their power and authority in evil, hurtful ways. Considering these challenges, I would like to invite you to join me in the transformative power of God's Word, allowing it to renew our minds and deepen our understanding of his sovereignty.

The Bible reveals God as the sovereign Creator, Sustainer, and Ruler. And while his greatness is awesome, his moral goodness is the essence of his beauty. Jonathan Edwards contrasts God's greatness with demons and fallen people. Demons are great, but they are evil. As a result, their power is terrifying. There have also been men and women throughout history who are great in power, yet due to corruption in their hearts, their greatness has been used to destroy many. But God is different because he is both great and morally excellent. As a result, the One who rules the world is *good* and works all things toward his *good* purposes!

PSALM 33:10-12 | ISAIAH 55:6-13

DISCUSS TOGETHER

3. How do our plans contrast with God's plans (Psalm 33:10-11)? In what areas of your life have you experienced the difference between your plans and God's plans?

4. How does God sovereignly work to bring about his good purposes (Isaiah 55:6-13)? How does this grow your understanding of God?

5. What are some other examples in Scripture of God sovereignly working to bring about good in people's lives?

6. Which passage of God's sovereign work in people's lives resonates with you the most? Why?

READ TOGETHER

Trust-filled submission to God. This week God's people will struggle with the revelation of his future plans. Certainly, we can relate! Sometimes we do not understand how God is unfolding the events in the world and in our lives. But God will teach us a new habit to live by so we can walk with trust-filled submission, even when we do not understand the work of his good hands. Let's prepare our hearts for Isaiah's message by looking at a man who also learned trust-filled submission to God's governance of the world.

JOB 42:1-6

DISCUSS TOGETHER

7. What did Job acknowledge about God and confess about himself? What can we learn from Job?

8. What is the significance of Job's confession taking place when he did not have "knowledge" and "did not understand" (v. 3)?

9. Why is it important for us to learn how to trust and submit to God even though we do not understand the work of his hand?

READ TOGETHER

He will uphold and carry you. Friend, I am excited for you to see the stunning conclusion to our study this week. After God lifts our eyes to see his global governance, he will remind us that he also upholds us! The flow of thought in the chapter reminds me of Isaiah's opening message in chapter 40, where God taught us to lift our eyes to the stars and remember: he is far greater than the things he has made, yet he is intimately involved in our lives.

10. When have you seen God uphold you? How did it lead you to worship God more?

11. How can your story be an encouragement to other people?

MANY PEOPLE TURN OFF THE NEWS today because tension is high. Escaping from the larger world seems comforting, yet we do not want to be people who cower

| FOR THE SAKE OF MY CHOSEN ISAIAH 44:21–45:8 | DAY 1 |

back in fear. So how can we find the courage to stay engaged in the world of chaos without falling into anxiety? In our passage today, God calls us to come out of our small, self-contained worlds to see the larger world around us. When we look at the world through his lenses, we find that the universe is God-contained! While it is undoubtedly a joy to enter the small, quiet life of novels and movies for a time, God teaches us how to remain courageously dialed in to the real world so we can be salt and light to others.

Read Isaiah 44:21–45:8. What do you observe?

● God calls his people to "Remember these things" (44:21). What does the Lord want his people to remember (vv. 21-28), and why is this important?

Though you don't know me. God's people should remember all the gracious works he did to forgive their sins and redeem them. He also wanted people to remember that he planned and predicted the Jews' deliverance long before it happened (44:21). The Lord revealed that a man named Cyrus would deliver the Jews, causing Jerusalem to be inhabited over 150 years in advance! And Isaiah 45:1-8 predicted the victories of Cyrus with amazing details that were literally fulfilled in time. The Lord "anointed" Cyrus—or set him apart for a special task—and gave him the *great* success we see in historical accounts.

● What success did God give Cyrus (vv. 1-8)? Why is it important for us to recognize that Cyrus's success was given to him by God?

It is fascinating to compare the biblical account of Cyrus with its fulfillment in history. Cyrus is remembered in history as one of the most benevolent conquerors of all time. He was born to royalty in 590 BC and became recognized early for his giftedness. After uniting the Iranian tribes, he formed an army and had great victories throughout Mesopotamia, collecting immense wealth from the treasuries of the conquered countries. The release of the Jews and the support he gave to them in rebuilding their temple is heralded as Cyrus's highest act of mercy.

For the sake of my chosen. Considering the extensive lengths God took to help his people is astonishing. Why did God do all this extraordinary work? He answers this question in Isaiah 45:4: for the sake of his chosen!

● Why did God do all the extraordinary work of raising a king and causing countries to fall (v. 4)? How does this grow your understanding of God's sovereignty?

After conquering many lands in Mesopotamia, God turned Cyrus's attention toward Babylon to deliver his people from captivity. For further study, you can read about the victory God gave Cyrus over Babylon in Daniel 5. Judgment came upon the king of Babylon, and his kingdom was given to Persia. The Persians defeated Babylon on October 12, 539 BC.

Paraphrase God's message.

“

”

 TRANSFORMING LIFE PRINCIPLE

When our world seems to unravel, we can rest knowing God is sovereignly weaving all things together for the good of his people.

● Every part of creation is under God's sovereign rule—all nations, people, and spiritual beings. How will these passages change your perspective when our world seems chaotic?

- How does God's extensive work for the sake of his people comfort you personally?

- In what specific ways can this passage comfort and encourage you to remain dialed in to the real world so you can be salt and light to others?

DAY 2 — THE POTTER AND THE CLAY
ISAIAH 45:9-13

HOW DO YOU PRESS THROUGH those days when you do not understand God's work in your life and are confused by how situations are unfolding? Some of us become deeply frustrated and angry with God. Others withdraw from him in discouragement and confusion. But what if we could shut down those dead-end roads in our soul? Are there truths in the Bible that can set our thoughts and emotions on a path of resting submissively in God's hands while we trust and wait for him to work all things together for good?

In our passage today, God anticipates objections by the Jews concerning his plan to deliver the nation using a Gentile king—who did not know God—and God's future plan to redeem both Jews and Gentiles. God responds to their arguments using the illustration of a potter and his clay, teaching us how to rest in him, even when we do not understand the work of his good hand.

 Read Isaiah 45:9-13. What do you observe?

● What does God teach his people not to do (vv. 9-10)? When has this been difficult for you?

● What does God command Israel to ask him (vv. 11-12)? What does this teach us about God?

● **God formed the earth and fashioned it.** The basic meaning of the Hebrew root word *yatsar* is "to shape or form." Scripture uses this word to describe God's work as the Creator of the heavens and the earth. "The LORD *formed* the man of dust from the ground and breathed into his nostrils the breath of life" (Genesis 2:7 italics added). God *formed* and fashioned the earth (Isaiah 45:18). He also *formed* Israel into a vessel for his glory (Isaiah 43:1, 7).

● What can we learn about God's authority by pondering and picturing him forming and fashioning creation? Why is this lesson important?

The potter and his clay. God was eager to tell the nation what he would do for them in the future. He would help the Jews return to Jerusalem and rebuild the temple through a man named Cyrus. But the Lord also anticipated their objections to his use of a Gentile king to deliver them. God responded to their arguments with the *illustration* of a potter. Interestingly, this is a picture often used in Scripture to address people who argue with their Creator about the work of his hands.

● Read Jeremiah 18:1-11, Isaiah 29:13-16, and Isaiah 64:1-12. How does the potter illustration in these passages help you understand God's message to the exiles?

Jeremiah 18:1-11

Isaiah 29:13-16

Isaiah 64:1-12

God told Jeremiah to go to the potter's house and watch him mold clay into pots. As the potter fashioned the clay, he found a flaw in the pot. So the potter pressed it back into a lump and formed it again into another vessel as it seemed best to him. God wanted his people to know that he is like a potter, and his sinful people were the clay. He can tear down and build up nations as he pleases. Though he gave Judah opportunities to repent, their refusal resulted in being torn down into a lump of clay so he could form something new.

Isaiah 64:8-12 gives us a glimpse into the future faith of a righteous remnant. After being refined in the furnace of affliction, God's people confessed their trust in God as a good Father and Potter. In other words, they learned how to find comfort in becoming submissive clay in God's good hands!

I am reminded of a woman who once shared her grief with me about the brokenness of her family. Many people in her family began walking with Christ later in life. And while they had individually grown to become more like Jesus, they would fall back into dysfunctional patterns when they were together.

After years of dysfunction, everything came crashing down in a single day. Sinful words from a family member resulted in the unraveling of one relationship, which led to the unraveling of other relationships as people took sides. The woman was confused. How can a family fall apart when many individuals believe in Jesus Christ? And why wasn't God answering her prayers to restore their family?

She found great comfort in our passage today. She began to realize that God was unraveling their sinful relationships in order to press the clay back into a lump to be formed into something new. In time she watched the Lord progressively restore their relationships into a family that reflected his glory. And the illustration set before us today taught her to surrender like submissive clay in the good potter's hand, trusting him to work in his higher ways.

Paraphrase God's message.

TRANSFORMING LIFE PRINCIPLE

When life's complexities confound us, find solace by surrendering to our loving and sovereign Father, as yielding clay rests in a potter's skilled hands.

● How do you often respond when you do not understand the work of the Lord in your life?

● What is a situation in your life where you need to acknowledge God as a good Father and Potter and trust his work like submissive clay?

● In what ways will picturing the potter and his clay provide comfort when you do not understand God's work in your life?

DAY 3	EVERY KNEE WILL BOW ISAIAH 45:14-25

THROUGHOUT THIS WEEK'S STUDY, God has guided our thoughts toward global affairs. And these enduring truths are timely! People are greatly divided by views of race, gender, religion, politics, and more. Voices are loud, and tensions are high. But Isaiah provides us with more comfort by transporting us to a time when all lies, deception, and power struggles will cease. The entire world will acknowledge one truth: Jesus Christ is Lord. I am eager to meet with you in our passage today to learn more habits for firing up our faith when the world seems dark and hopeless.

Read Isaiah 45:14-25.

● Isaiah opens by using three countries as illustrations of worldwide submission to Israel's God in the future (v. 14). How do the nations express their submission to God? How should these expressions shape and influence us?

● What distinctions does God make between himself and substitute gods (vv. 16-21)? How do these distinctions teach people to turn to the One true God?

● To whom is God directing his message and what is the essence of his message (vv. 22-23)? How should this profound revelation lead us to respond in worship and awe?

Let us go with you! When God liberated the Jewish captives and sent them home, some Babylonians sought to join themselves with Israel's extraordinary God. The Lord called people to reject their idols and turn to him, and some responded to his call of repentance. As a result, the restoration of the Jews resulted in the conversion of people from other nations! In Zechariah 8, the prophet takes us forward in time, describing the restoration of the exiles to their land.

● Read Zechariah 8:20-23. How does this passage provide a preview of God's future plan to redeem both Jews and Gentiles? What does this reveal about God?

● Why will people from different nations want to "go with" the Jews to their God (v. 23)? How should God's inclusive plan for all nations motivate and inspire us to actively share the gospel with the people in our lives?

A global confession coming soon. In Philippians 2:10-11, the apostle Paul quoted Isaiah. He used a literary device called *threefold articulation* to repeat and emphasize the extent of Christ's sovereign authority, which I have highlighted in the verse below:

> Therefore God has highly exalted him and bestowed on him the name that is above every name, so that at the name of Jesus every knee should bow, *in heaven and on earth and under the earth*, and every tongue confess that Jesus Christ is Lord, to the glory of God the Father.

Today, many Gentiles hear the gospel and joyfully bend their knee to Jesus Christ as their personal Lord and Savior—me included! However, when Christ returns in all his glory, even unbelievers will acknowledge his lordship—though they will do so as rebels conquered by the King. After all things are brought into submission to the Lord, he will manifest his kingdom throughout the world, and we will praise him as our Prince of Peace. And that, my friend, is a message of hope to stand on when we feel discouraged by today's broken and chaotic world.

TRANSFORMING LIFE PRINCIPLE

We can face chaos in our world with hope and purpose by engaging in gospel ministry and eagerly anticipating the triumphant return of Jesus Christ.

● Reflect on the universe of angels, demons, believers, and unbelievers bowing before Jesus. How can this change your perspective when you become anxious about living in a tumultuous world?

● What are some obstacles to having spiritual conversations and sharing the gospel with the people in your life?

● Philip shared the gospel using Isaiah. Take a moment to read the guide "How to Share the Gospel in Isaiah" in the back of this study. How can this equip you to have gospel conversations?

EVEN TO YOUR OLD AGE
ISAIAH 46

THERE ARE TIMES THROUGHOUT THE DAY when life presses heavily upon us. We all have those moments—when an email comes through from work with a problem that needs to be solved, your child begins to cry because of a hard day at school, or the phone rings with the news that your aging parent has been in a car wreck. Where do you turn to for hope and help when the pressures of life fall heavily on your shoulders? Some people snap, and others fall into despair. Some dig deeper to find more strength within themselves, and others look frantically for help apart from God. But the Lord gives us a glorious alternative in our passage today. In Isaiah 46, God brings his rebuke of idols to a close by making a final contrast: idols place burdens on the backs of their worshipers, but God carries the burdens of his people.

 Read Isaiah 46.

● How does God describe his burden-bearing love (vv. 1-4)? What does this teach us about God?

● What works did God do on Israel's behalf (vv. 8-9)? How does this give abundant evidence that He alone is God?

The heavy burdens of idolatry. We have seen God graciously battle for the hearts of his people throughout Isaiah. In our passage today, God refers to Babylon's gods by name. Bel refers to Marduk, the supreme deity of Babylon, and Nebo was his son. Both were beloved gods of the Assyrian-Babylonian pantheon. Nebo was the god of learning; his symbols were the clay tablet and the stylus. A statue of him is in the British Museum. Interestingly, the kings of Babylon took the names of their gods within their titles. So, for example, Bel's name went into Belshazzar and Nebo into Nebuchadnezzar.

Some believed the Babylonian gods were more powerful than Judah's God since the Jews were in captivity. But now that God's discipline of the Jews had ended, he would show himself to the Babylonians as the Defender of his people and the One true God. "Bel bows down; Nebo stoops," and "they . . . themselves go into captivity" refer to God's coming destruction of Babylon's idols.

> *Cast your burden on the Lord, and he will sustain you; he will never permit the righteous to be moved.*
>
> **PSALM 55:22**

They leave you weak and weary. God masterfully uses mockery to contrast the burdens idols place on people's backs with the One who carries the burdens of his people. The prophet also gives us a powerful picture to illustrate the impotence of idols. Graven images were carried on the backs of horses and mules. The idols were covered with silver and gold, weighing them down and making them heavy to carry.

God used this illustration to teach people that idols are a burden to the weary. The primary meaning of the word *weary* is "exhausted in strength, endurance, vigor, or freshness." Did you catch the point of God's mockery? When we turn to substitutes for God, we will become like mules who are left carrying our burdens! Friend, this is a powerful truth to remember. One indicator that we are drifting from our trust in God is weariness from trying to carry our burdens.

- What does God's use of mockery teach us about the nature of idolatry? How can remembering this truth change our mindset during temptation?

Even to old age, I will carry you. God transitions from the helplessness of idols to some of my favorite expressions of his love. Isaiah uses a maternal *metaphor* to illustrate God's concern and care for his people. The Lord is said to have given birth to Israel (Deuteronomy 32:18). He has helped and nurtured the nations since he created them. And then, he follows the birth metaphor with an *image* of gray hair to communicate God's lifelong commitment to his people! The root Hebrew root word *sabal* is translated as "to carry" and means "to bear a load." Even in our old age, God will carry us and bear our heavy loads.

● How does picturing and pondering the images of God's lifelong commitment comfort God's people?

The Lord speaks a precious message to us today. Some of us are beginning the season of caring more for our aging parents. Others of us may be feeling unsettled by the aging process in our own lives. When our sight begins to fail, we can find comfort in knowing God has not lost sight of us. When our mobility decreases, we can trust that God will carry us. When the fear of falling becomes a real threat, we can rest knowing God will uphold us. When it is time to relinquish the baton of leadership, we can look forward to the epic and eternal adventures to come. And when death becomes a daily prospect, we can trust that God will bring us safely home. Many people fail to honor and help the aged. But God will rise to take their place, "To whom will you liken me and make me equal, and compare me, that we may be alike?" (Isaiah 46:5).

TRANSFORMING LIFE PRINCIPLE

As the years pass, God's loving arms remain a refuge, bearing our heavy loads with unwavering care.

- When you feel the weight of your heavy burdens, what idols or substitutes for God are you prone to turn to for comfort and help? How do these idols leave you weary from carrying your burdens?

- In what specific ways have you been led to love and appreciate God more today?

- How are you personally comforted by God's promise to carry you even through old age?

IN OUR STUDY THIS WEEK, the Lord led us to higher places, giving us a glimpse of his governance of the world. We can trust

CHRIST'S BURDEN-BEARING GRACE

DAY 5

that he is sovereignly working all things together for the good of his people. Even when we do not understand the way things are unfolding, we can find comfort by trusting the potter's work like submissive clay. And we can look with confidence to the future when all things will be brought into submission to Jesus Christ, confessing him as Lord. After teaching us global truths that will strengthen us to walk through difficult days on a global level, he comes back down to our small lives with a stunning message: the One who upholds the world also upholds us! He concluded with another call to turn from idols that leave us carrying our own burdens and turn to the One who delights to carry our burdens. Today, we will reflect on even higher expressions of God's burden-bearing grace revealed in the New Testament!

READ

He bore our iniquities. The Hebrew root word *sabal*, "to bear a load," is also used in contexts for *bearing* the punishment or penalty for sin. In Lamentations 5:7, the Israelites grieved that they had sinned by breaking the covenant with God and must *bear* the punishment in exile. But God's burden-bearing love comes to a climax in Isaiah 53. The coming servant of the Lord will *bear* the sickness and sorrow of his people's sin and the penalty that must be paid. Jesus Christ fulfilled this prophecy, bearing our sin and punishment on the cross. What is the result of his burden-bearing sacrifice? Though believers experience temporal discipline to teach us righteousness, we will never bear the punishment for our sin!

ISAIAH 53:1-11

REFLECT

● Jesus Christ demonstrated a higher fulfillment of God's burden-bearing love for you. Why does this lead you to love and adore him more today?

READ

Come to me, I will give you rest. The New Testament gives us a fuller picture of God's compassion and care for the weak and weary. Jesus sees the heavy loads on moms, students, employees, gospel ministers, and more. He has compassion on us. And he makes a beautiful gospel call to us all: "Come to me, all who labor and are heavy laden, and I will give you rest." Interestingly, Nebo was the Babylonian god of learning, but his tutelage left worshipers carrying their own heavy burdens. In contrast, Jesus invites us to learn from him and walk in his burden-lifting grace.

MATTHEW 11:28-30

REFLECT

- Are there any particular burdens or worries that you've been hesitant to surrender to Jesus? What might be holding you back from fully embracing his offer of rest?

READ

Bear with one another. As image bearers, we are privileged to know Jesus Christ and *become* like him. But there are times when being like Jesus is challenging. You may agree that the call to bear with one another is one of those times. Sin is selfish and offensive. It leads people to explode with anger. It is malicious, taking pleasure in being mean-spirited for no reason. Sin says hurtful things; it tears people down and oversteps boundaries. Sin is blind to its wrongdoings and hypocritical in its judgments of others. In short, sin is exhausting, and it can feel like a heavy burden to bear with one another.

But we are not without help. God gives us Jesus Christ as our model and the Holy Spirit to empower us for life and godliness. As we have seen throughout this study, God is in the midst of his people, strengthening the humble, weakening the proud, and refining his people. We can bear with one another, forgiving each other as Christ has forgiven us, knowing the Lord will continue to sanctify his bride until he returns to present us without spot or blemish!

Colossians 3:12-14 | Ephesians 4:1-7

REFLECT

- What steps can you take to bear with someone in your life? Ask the Holy Spirit to help and empower you.

Rest

Knowing that God is sovereign—upholding and guiding the universe—we can confidently entrust him with all our concerns. Because Jesus offers us rest from the many things that weigh down our hearts and minds, take some time to list those many cares here and surrender them to him.

YOU KEEP HIM IN PERFECT PEACE WHOSE MIND IS STAYED ON YOU, BECAUSE HE TRUSTS IN YOU. TRUST IN THE LORD FOREVER, FOR THE LORD GOD IS AN EVERLASTING ROCK.

ISAIAH 26:3-4

WEEK SIX | WALK RIGHTEOUSLY

Who are some of your role models? When we see a person display beauty, strength, and success, we can be motivated to emulate their ways. One inspiring role model presented to us in the Bible is Daniel—a man who was devoted to God and walked righteously during difficult days. Daniel was a light to his fellow exiles during the Babylonian captivity and was used by God in extraordinary ways. I am eager to show you that many of Daniel's successes flowed from walking in the catalog of comforts given to us in Isaiah 40–48! I cannot think of a better transition into our last week of study than to see how Daniel's life displays some of the lessons we have learned thus far and how he also put into practice the lessons we will

 discover this week. Then we will close our time with final reflections on our six-week study together!

View the week six video to begin this group session.

READ TOGETHER

Walk righteously during difficult days. Can you imagine being deported from your homeland and placed in captivity? It would be terrifying to lose our freedom and be taken to a foreign land. Surely, we would be tempted to shrink from God's ways to escape persecution and find rest in sinful forms of comfort. In this week's passages, God tells his people that their peace would have been like a river if they had followed his righteous instructions. Though the nation failed, the book of Daniel introduces us to a man who was part of a righteous remnant of Jews. Daniel chose peace with God rather than peace with the Babylonians and walking in their godless ways. He remained devoted to the Lord during the Babylonian captivity, becoming an example to the exiles and us today.

DANIEL 6:1-5

DISCUSS TOGETHER

1. What words are used to distinguish Daniel as a man who lived righteously? How can we develop these characteristics?

2. What are some ways believers are tempted to refrain from speaking and representing God's ways to avoid persecution today? How can Daniel's life encourage us to walk righteously during difficult days?

READ TOGETHER

Be a witness for God. Throughout our study, we have learned that God called Israel to be his witness to the nations. Daniel walked with God and was used as his witness to the Babylonians. One place we see this is in Daniel chapter 1. After we are introduced to Daniel's devotion to God (vv. 8-16), we see that Daniel was used mightily for the Lord (vv. 17-21).

DANIEL 1:17-21

DISCUSS TOGETHER

3. In what ways did God honor Daniel's trust and allegiance to him (vv. 17-21)? How does this serve as a word of encouragement to us?

4. How did the Lord use Daniel as a witness? Why does Daniel's faithfulness to God matter?

READ TOGETHER

Trust God to help his people. Throughout Isaiah 40–48, God teaches us to
be confident in his help. He has a special love for those in a covenant
relationship with him. Sometimes God delivers us from hardship. Other
times, he sustains and upholds us through adversity: "When you pass
through the waters, I will be with you" (Isaiah 43:2). Daniel continued to
pray to God even though the law forbade it, and he was thrown into a lion's
den to be devoured. But let's consider how God upheld Daniel.

   DANIEL 6:16-28

DISCUSS TOGETHER

5. In what ways did God help Daniel through the lion's den? How should
   God's faithfulness encourage us?

6. Where do you need to trust God for help? What difference can trusting
   God make in your situation?

READ TOGETHER

Believe God's Word. Through our study, we have learned that God gave us prophecy to strengthen our faith in his promises and to give us a hopeful perspective. We see Daniel model this practice! After sixty-six years of captivity, Daniel was studying "the books" or Old Testament scrolls, focusing on Jeremiah's prophecy that the Jews would be disciplined for seventy years (Jeremiah 25:11-12). Perceiving—and believing—that their captivity was nearing its end, Daniel confessed the sin of the Jewish nation that resulted in exile and interceded for them, asking God to set them free from Babylonian captivity. Within a few years, the Lord fulfilled his promise made through Jeremiah, answering Daniel's prayer by stirring up the king of Persia to deliver his people!

DANIEL 9:1-19

DISCUSS TOGETHER

7. What spiritual disciplines did Daniel do to seek the Lord (vv. 1-6)? How does his example provide a model for us?

8. What aspect of Daniel's example in exile challenges and encourages you? Why?

FINAL REFLECTIONS TOGETHER ON ISAIAH

9. What was most noteworthy to you about the trustworthiness of God in Isaiah? How has it grown your ability to trust God to help and uphold you?

10. What theme in Isaiah 40–48 was the most meaningful to you? Why?

11. Which passage will you use to put off fear and put on faith in God? What situation will this be helpful to you?

12. What passage in Isaiah would you like to memorize? How would memorizing it transform your life?

SIT IN THE DUST

ISAIAH 47

IT CAN BE HARD TO SEE PEOPLE "get away" with wickedness. We can find ourselves wondering, *Will the wicked be able to build forever?* Our heart may ask a similar question to Habakkuk, "O Lord, how long shall I cry for help, and you will not hear? Or cry to you 'Violence!' and you will not save?" (Habakkuk 1:2). As our culture increasingly opposes God and his ways, our societies, schools, workplaces, and other communities will become more unloving and oppressive. Like Lot, believers in Jesus Christ will be troubled by the perversion around us. Like Noah, we will be persecuted for walking in righteousness. But like Judah, we will be given relief by God.

In our passage today, God reminds Judah that he gave them into the hands of the Babylonians to be refined because of their wicked ways and refusal to repent. But their captivity was ending, and now God would judge the wickedness of their oppressor. As we study God's Word together, we will learn how to find comfort and relief in our just God while we walk through difficult days.

 Read Isaiah 47. What stands out to you?

● Why will Babylon be judged (v. 6)? What does this reveal about God's justice?

● What are the expressions of Babylon's arrogance (vv. 7-15)? What lessons about pride can we glean from their example?

● Babylon leaned heavily on astrologers and magical practices (vv. 12-15). How does their outcome shift our mindset when we are tempted to rely on someone or something other than God?

The city of rebellion. Through Isaiah, we learn that God used Babylon to humble his hardened and unrepentant people. Interestingly, Babylon is known in the Bible as the city of rebellion. It is first mentioned in Genesis 11, when fallen and prideful people united to build the tower of Babel "with its top in the heavens." The people attempted to rise to the place of God, determining what was right in their own eyes. God judged their pride by confusing their language, forcing them to fulfill his mandate to multiply and spread throughout the world.

Let's consider the significance of God's scattering work on a small scale to help us understand the importance of Genesis 11. Have you ever seen school culture where mean girls or aggressive boys gravitate together, uniting into one entity to bully and control others? As they grow in numbers, it is difficult for the righteous or nonconformists to stand against them. I have seen God bring relief to children and parents by scattering some of these groups so they cannot be strengthened in their ungodly ways. Now let's consider this scenario globally, and we will better understand Babel. God's judgment on Babel prevented prideful people from uniting into one entity in their rebellion against God, making space and time for his plan of salvation to be worked out.

A taunt song. Isaiah described Babylon's arrogance as being lovers of pleasure and sitting securely on their throne, singing songs about trusting in magic spells, sorceries, and horoscopes. But now that God's judgment has arrived, Israel will sing a song about the tragedy of sinners to their oppressor. Isaiah used more *imagery* to help us ponder and picture God's work of judgment. The Lord spoke using symbolic words of judgment, "Come down and sit in the dust, . . . sit on the ground without a throne" (v. 1) and "Sit in silence, and go into darkness" (v. 5).

● Pause to ponder and picture these images in your mind. How do these symbolic images grow your understanding of God's judgment?

This lesson is certainly relevant today! There are loud cries for justice worldwide. Many of the topics driving conversations are centered on people seeking justice for having been hurt by individuals or groups of people. Isaiah teaches us some principles for finding comfort in God, his greater purposes, and his love for justice. The Lord is working all things together for the good of his people. He gives his people relief by judging wicked people each day. And he will give us eternal relief on the final day of judgment. With this in mind, God calls us to continue participating in gospel work—leading people to repent of their sins and be reconciled to him before that great and final day!

TRANSFORMING LIFE PRINCIPLE

Amid the growing opposition to God and his ways, believers can take heart knowing his coming judgment will result in worldwide peace and relief.

● What situations in your life or our world today have awakened a longing for justice in your heart?

● How does God's coming judgment on the fallen and oppressive world systems comfort you?

● What is your greatest takeaway from these passages?

WHERE ARE YOU IN YOUR JOURNEY of embracing the Lord's discipline as a Father's loving involvement in your life? To be honest, I struggled for many years—feeling discouraged

REFINED LIKE GOLD
ISAIAH 48:1-11

DAY 2

during seasons of affliction and discipline. Perhaps you can relate when I say my mind needed to be transformed to continue walking with a hopeful view of the holy harvest to come—even when the process is unpleasant. One way to grow in a more mature mindset is to reflect on God's good heart and the purpose behind discipline. In Isaiah 48, the Lord reminded Judah that he brought them through the fires of affliction to refine them. And through this passage, we can glean principles to stand on during these unpleasant seasons. *Lord, teach us to find comfort in you . . . even when you refine us!*

 Read Isaiah 48:1-11.

● What were the expressions of Israel's obstinacy and hypocrisy (vv. 1-2)? What does their example teach us about God's view of nominal Israelites or Christians? (Nominal means being something in name only because there is no true heart in it).

● Why did God help Judah, even though the nation deserved wrath and punishment (vv. 9-11)? What does this reveal about God?

(For further study, read Isaiah 1 to discover more about the spiritual condition of Israel that led to God's discipline.)

God's rebuke of Judah would have been hard to hear. And certainly, we can relate. No one is eager for their sin to be confronted. But have you ever considered that many others see our sin while we refuse to acknowledge it? Refusing to look at our sin is like walking around with food in our teeth. Everyone sees it, but some do not tell us because they don't want to embarrass us. So we continue walking through the room smiling and having a good ol' time while everyone is looking at the food in our teeth (laughing as I write).

But seriously, the woman who always corrects people because she wants to be seen as intelligent doesn't understand why people don't stay long conversing with her. The woman with boundary issues doesn't understand why people aren't excited when she visits. The woman who is bitter and critical wonders why she is often alone. We often see the consequences of our sins but lack the courage or spiritual sight to trace the fruit back to the root in our heart. But let's choose together to have a different disposition toward our sin and God's purifying work in our lives.

The words of the Lord are pure words, like silver refined in a furnace on the ground, purified seven times.

PSALM 12:6

I will refine you like gold.

The Lord put Israel through affliction to refine them (v. 10). The Hebrew root word *tsaraph* describes goldsmiths, silversmiths, and the process of *refining* metals to be shaped into fine vessels. God frequently uses the *imagery* of a smith refining metal to describe his work of purifying people from sin. When metals are heated, pure metal is poured and fashioned into a fine vessel. The residue left is the dross or impurities, which are skimmed off. God refines his people so they can walk in holiness and be used by him.

● Read Psalm 66:8-12, Jeremiah 6:27-30, and Isaiah 26:9-11. How do these passages help you understand humanity's different responses to God's refining work? Which one do you relate with the most and why?

Psalm 66:8-12

Jeremiah 6:27-30

Isaiah 26:9-11

● Read Isaiah 1:24-26 and Isaiah 4:2-6. What do these passages teach us about the outcome of God's refining work? How can these verses encourage us during seasons of hardship?

Isaiah 1:24-26

Isaiah 4:2-6

Some people are so stubborn that they will go through seasons of God's discipline in vain and come out unchanged! But God teaches us to humble ourselves, recognizing his gracious purpose and the good results of refinement. We can patiently endure his training by remembering it is not condemnation. Our loving Father is preparing us to participate in the family glory and to rule with Christ in the age to come. And when we walk by faith, we will emerge from the fire of affliction refined like gold!

TRANSFORMING LIFE PRINCIPLE
We can walk through the fires of affliction with faith, knowing we will emerge like gold.

● What statement resonated with you the most today and why?

● How have these passages changed your perspective of God's discipline?

● In what specific ways can pondering and picturing the image of being refined like gold comfort you during seasons of hardship?

WHEN YOU THINK ABOUT AREAS IN YOUR LIFE where there is a lack of peace, is there also a lack of obedience to God? To be clear, there is not always a direct correlation between

PEACE LIKE A RIVER
ISAIAH 48:12-19

DAY 3

struggle and personal sin. Like Jesus, suffering will sometimes befall us because we *are* walking in righteousness. But there are areas of self-inflicted pain in many of our lives. Some of us lack financial peace because we are not stewarding our finances according to Christ's ways. Others may lack peace in our relationships because we are not walking in the humble and selfless ways of Christ. Others may lack peace in our sense of purpose because we seek worldly comfort, wealth, and renown instead of Christ's kingdom and righteousness.

In Isaiah 48, God reminds Judah that *if* the nation had walked in his ways, *then* their peace would have been like a river and their righteousness like the waves of the sea. Now that their liberation has come, God reminds his people to listen and learn his ways to be restored to righteousness, peace, and wholeness in their land.

Read Isaiah 48:12-19.

● What do you observe about God's promise of deliverance (vv. 12-16)? What stands out to you the most and why?

● List the rewards Judah forfeited because they did not listen and learn from the Lord (vv. 17-19). How do these verses affect the way you think about obedience to God?

Learn how to profit spiritually. Isaiah used the *image* of a river to describe the peace that flows through individuals and societies who walk in God's good ways. And while the picture of a river speaks powerfully to all our imaginations, it would have been even more striking to God's original audience because major rivers flowed throughout the Bible lands.

● Picture and ponder a river of peace. How does this metaphor enhance your understanding of listening to and applying God's teachings to our lives?

One of the greatest blessings of being part of God's people is learning his ways. Throughout their existence as a nation, God taught Israel and instructed them. We saw the effects of righteousness for a short time following King David's reign when peace, or shalom, filled their land.

But it is tragic to read the Lord's words to Judah in our passage today: *if* they had listened, *then* their peace would have been like a river and their righteousness like the waves of the sea. Instead, God's people were like stubborn heifers, refusing to pay attention to his instructions, which led to their destruction and exile (Hosea 10:11). But now their time of discipline was ending. God reminded them to listen and learn from him.

● Take a moment to reflect on Judah's fall from peace due to their rejection of God's instructions. Why do we often emulate Israel by departing from God's Word?

One reason I often see myself and others exchanging God's instructions for the world's wisdom is that we lean on our own understanding. In 1 Corinthians, the apostle Paul teaches that human wisdom is centered on pride. Worldly wisdom puts the self at the center of our motivations, pursuits, and end goals. For this reason, it often makes more sense to coach our children to do things that put them at an advantage in school and their social circles rather than to teach them to humble themselves and serve others. Building security with our resources can make more sense to us than using them for God's kingdom. I could roll on with examples in relationships, marriage, leadership methods, and more. But the point is this: we often climb out of the river of peace because we lean on our own understanding, which can be contrary to God's wisdom and ways.

Good and upright is the Lord; therefore, he instructs sinners in the way.

PSALM 25:8

Through our passage today, we learn another habit for walking in God's comfort. When we are devoted learners of Jesus—people who do not merely hear his Word but apply it to our lives—we will remain in the peace of Christ and find our hearts singing, *It is well with my soul.*

TRANSFORMING LIFE PRINCIPLE

The journey of discipleship leads to peace like a river deep in our soul and righteousness flowing like the waves of the sea.

● In what specific ways have you experienced peace and spiritual prosperity by applying Christ's instructions to your life?

● List one area of your life that is lacking peace. When you lay that area next to God's instructions in Scripture, does it align with his wisdom, or have you stepped away from obedience to God?

● What action steps can you take to walk in obedience to Christ?

AFTER MOVING TO HOUSTON, I visited Galveston Island, a beach town enjoyed by many Texans. As we drove along the sandy shores and took in all the

historic architecture, I heard fascinating stories from its past, including one that has stuck with me throughout the years. In the 1860s, one-third of Galveston's population lived under the oppression of slavery. But on June 19, 1865, Union soldiers arrived in Galveston to announce that slavery had been abolished in the United States. Good news, right? If you know historical dates, you may have noticed a time lapse between the arrival of the Union soldiers and Abraham Lincoln's Emancipation Proclamation on January 1, 1863. For two and a half years, the slaves in Galveston remained in bondage even though they were free!

Can you relate to this story on a spiritual level? I certainly can! As believers in Jesus Christ, we have been set free from slavery to our sin. Our old, fallen self died with Christ. And we have been raised to walk in a new life with him. And yet, many of us remain in various forms of bondage. Perhaps your past traumas and fears still control you. Or perhaps your old identities still define you. Or maybe remnant sin still has a hold on you. In Isaiah 48, Judah's liberation had come. And through our passage today, God will teach us new habits for overcoming the temptation to fall back into our old patterns of bondage.

 Read Isaiah 48:20-22.

● What does God call his people to do (v. 20)? How does God's work of redemption enable his people to respond in these ways?

● What help did God provide for Israel when he redeemed them from
   Egypt (v. 21)? How would the illustration of the exodus from Egypt stir
   up faith to separate from Babylon and return home?

Proclaim redemption to the ends of the earth. After stirring in the
heart of Cyrus, God proclaimed freedom to his people, telling them
to leave Babylon! It is important to recognize that redemption is a gift from
God; he does all the work necessary for the salvation of his people. But it is
also important to understand the response he calls forth from his people.
Let's look at these responses together.

Isaiah used the poetic device of *allusion*—a reference to a past event
designed to stir up familiar thoughts and emotions in his reader's minds. *Go
out, flee, joy,* and *redeemed* echoed God's great deliverance during the first
exodus. Let's look at the allusions Isaiah makes to the Israelites' deliverance
from Egypt.

Read Exodus 13:3, 14:5, 15:1, and 20:2. Why are each of the responses
below appropriate for people redeemed by the Lord?

● *Exodus 13:3-8: Going out and going forth* is a significant theme from the
   first Exodus, emphasizing the benevolent work of God, who brought his
   people out of captivity. Isaiah tells the Jews to "go out" from Babylon
   into their freedom.

● *Exodus 14:5*: *Flee* describes one's flight from an enemy. The first exodus was described as a flight from Egypt. Isaiah echoed the command to "flee" Babylon.

● *Exodus 15:1*: Israel experienced great joy and celebration in God's redemption. Now Isaiah tells his people to shout with joy and proclaim their redemption.

Biblical *joy* is so fascinating that we must pause and marvel together. The Hebrew root *ranan* is *not* developed in the other Semitic languages. It is a Hebrew concept that describes the jubilation or joy of God's people in response to his saving acts on their behalf. Pause and marvel with me that joy belongs to the people of God!

The frequent use of the word shows that joy was to characterize and distinguish God's people. As I reflect on this beautiful truth today, I am reminded of how our old traumas, past bondages, and remnant sin can attempt to rob us of the joy of redemption. But let's continue to fight for our joy each morning by wrestling in the power of the Holy Spirit to put off the old and go forth in the new. And it will not be long, dear friend, until we experience the fullness of joy in the presence of the Lord forevermore!

TRANSFORMING LIFE PRINCIPLE

We will experience the comfort of redemption by coming out of past bondage, fleeing sin, and rejoicing in our new life with Christ!

The great "going out" event foreshadowed God's greater work of setting captives free from sin through Jesus Christ. Let's grow in experiencing God's gift of redemption by applying these three principles to our lives each day!

● What is an area of your life where you have remained in bondage even though you have been set free by faith in Christ?

● Can you identify some truths from our passages today that will empower you to progressively "come out" of past bondage and experience more freedom in Christ?

● What action steps must you take to "flee" a specific form of temptation in your life?

● Pause to ponder God's work of redemption in your life. What makes you want to rejoice, sing, and shout for joy? Let's close our time by communicating our gratitude to God through prayer.

As we wrap up our study on Isaiah, we can see why it is called the Gospel of the Old Testament! Students of the Bible have observed that Isaiah 40 begins with a cry in the wilderness, proclaiming the good news of deliverance from bondage to Babylon. And the book ends with Isaiah looking forward to the new heaven and new earth. Similarly, the New Testament begins with the voice of John the Baptist in the wilderness proclaiming the good news that Jesus Christ, the Messiah, has come to save his people from the bondage of sin. And the book of Revelation closes with God's redeemed bride and a new heaven and earth.

REDEEM THE TIME!

DAY 5

After reflecting on our salvation and *grand* future, our hearts may ask, *What should I do with the time I have left?* The New Testament instructs us to redeem our time because the days are evil (Ephesians 5:16). In other words, we should steward our remaining time to glorify God. With this in mind, I would like to show you two ways Isaiah 48 is fulfilled in Jesus Christ, which summarizes what God has called us to do in these last days. Then we will conclude with some final reflections together.

Freedom in Christ's redemption. In our passages this week, we studied the great "going out" event from Babylon. The Lord redeemed Judah and instructed them to *leave* Babylon. In a far greater way, Jesus Christ completed the work necessary for our salvation. The gospel calls us to repent by *leaving* our sin and beginning a new life with Jesus Christ. The Lord also told the redeemed Israelites to publish the good news of their liberation "to the end of the earth" (Isaiah 48:20). In the New Testament, Jesus clothes his disciples with the power of the Holy Spirit and sends us out to publish the good news of our liberation "to the end of the earth" (Acts 1:8). And just as God called the Israelites to joy, he instructs believers to rejoice always (1 Thessalonians 5:16-18). May we marvel at the unity of the Bible and the higher experience of redemption given to us today!

Follow Me. In Isaiah 48, the Lord revealed his delight in teaching sinners his ways. The New Testament Gospels present a beautiful portrait of Jesus gathering his beloved disciples, who referred to him as Rabbi, which means teacher. When they asked the teacher where he was staying, Jesus responded, "Come and you will see" (John 1:38-39). What a glorious picture of discipleship! Jesus calls us to use the time we have left to grow in our relationship with him. And we are also called to be part of the great mission to make disciples (Matthew 28:18-20). Jesus has authorized us to share the gospel with the people in our homes, workplaces, neighborhoods, churches, and other communities. And he promises to be with us, upholding us every step of the way!

FINAL REFLECTIONS ON THE FRUITFULNESS OF YOUR STUDY

● God's love for his people is steadfast and unchanging. How have you grown in putting off fear and putting on trust in God's promise to uphold you?

● The uniqueness of God is a significant theme in Isaiah—there is none like him! As you reflect on our study, how have you grown in your devotion to the Lord?

● Jesus is the fulfillment of the Law and Prophets. All of history pointed forward to him. How has the unity between the Old and New Testaments changed your reading of the Bible?

●   In Isaiah 40–48, God gives us a catalog of comforts for the different struggles we face each day. What promises of comfort have been the most life-changing for you?

As we come to the end of our journey, I want to thank you for joining me in God's Word. It has been an absolute joy meeting our trustworthy God in Isaiah together! May the lessons we have learned continue to uphold you, reminding you of God's faithfulness and unfailing love. And may we carry with us the resounding anthem that arose from our study: *Who is like the Lord? There is no God like him!*

IMAGES IN ISAIAH TO MEDITATE ON

- Spirituality white as snow

- Fading flowers and God's eternal Word

- Carried close to the Shepherd's heart

- God knows every star by name

- Strength mounting up with wings like eagles

- Upheld by God's hand

- Used like a strong instrument of God

- Renewed like springs in the desert

- Christ is gentle toward faintly burning wicks

- The Potter's purpose for his clay

- Refined into glorious metal

- Peace like a river

SIX HABITS TO EXCHANGE FEAR FOR CONFIDENCE IN GOD'S CARE

1. Turn to God for comfort.

2. Trade fear for faith.

3. Live the gospel.

4. Rest in God's grace.

5. Lean on the Sustainer.

6. Walk righteously.

OVERCOMING TEMPTATION

1

Pause.

From moving forward

2

Ponder,
picture, pray.

*Truths and images
in Isaiah*

4

Put on.

*A response that flows
from trust in God's promises*

3

Put off.

Sinful attitudes and actions

HOW TO SHARE THE GOSPEL IN ISAIAH

Isaiah 53:6 *Sin*	All we like sheep have gone astray; we have turned—every one—to his own way; and the LORD has laid on him the iniquity of us all.
Isaiah 64:6 *Spiritual depravity*	We have all become like one who is unclean, and all our righteous deeds are like a polluted garment. We all fade like a leaf, and our iniquities, like the wind, take us away.
Isaiah 53:5 *Christ's sacrifice*	But he was pierced for our transgressions; he was crushed for our iniquities; upon him was the chastisement that brought us peace, and with his wounds we are healed.
Isaiah 52:7 *Gospel presentation*	How beautiful upon the mountains are the feet of him who brings good news, who publishes peace, who brings good news of happiness, who publishes salvation, who says to Zion, "Your God reigns."
Isaiah 55:1 *Gospel invitation*	Come, everyone who thirsts, come to the waters; and he who has no money, come, buy and eat! Come, buy wine and milk without money and without price.
Isaiah 61:1 *Christ's mission*	The Spirit of the Lord GOD is upon me, because the LORD has anointed me to bring good news to the poor; he has sent me to bind up the brokenhearted, to proclaim liberty to the captives, and the opening of the prison to those who are bound.

Adoring Christ

Kori de Leon is the Founding Director of Adoring Christ Ministries, located in Houston, Texas.

If *Upheld* has encouraged and equipped you, we invite you to connect with Kori through additional resources and events.

Adoring Christ Ministries exists to bring women and teens into a transformative relationship with Jesus Christ—helping you believe in Jesus, behold Jesus, and become like him in all areas of life through

- podcasts
- Adoring Christ conferences
- EquipHer writer and speaker training
- books, Bible studies, and resources

For more information about Adoring Christ Ministries, visit www.adoringchrist.org.